Topics in Context

Context

Speaking of English

Themenheft

Cornelsen

Context
Speaking of English

Im Auftrag des Verlages herausgegeben von
Dr. Annette Leithner-Brauns, Dresden

Erarbeitet von
Martina Baasner, Berlin; Irene Bartscherer, Bonn; Lisa Braun, Meppen; Dr. Sabine Buchholz, Hürth; Wiebke Bettina Dietrich, Göttingen; Sylvia Loh, Esslingen; Benjamin Lorenz, Bensheim; Dr. Paul Maloney, Hildesheim; Dr. Pascal Ohlmann, Tholey; Birgit Ohmsieder, Berlin; Dr. Andreas Sedlatschek, Esslingen; Veronika Walther, Rudolstadt

In Zusammenarbeit mit der Englischredaktion
Dr. Marion Kiffe (Koordinierende Redakteurin), Dr. Christiane Kallenbach (Projektleitung), Aryane Beaudoin, Dr. Jan Dreßler, Hartmut Tschepe, Dr. Christian von Raumer, Freya Wurm *unter Mitwirkung von* Janan Barksdale, Irja Fröhling, Katrin Gütermann, Anne Müller, Neil Porter, Evelyn Sternad, Mai Weber

Beratende Mitwirkung
Ramin Azadian, Berlin; Heiko Benzin, Neustrelitz; Sabine Otto, Halle (Saale)

Layoutkonzept
Klein & Halm, Berlin

Layout und technische Umsetzung
Straive
designcollective, Berlin

Umschlaggestaltung
Rosendahl, Berlin

Lizenzmanagement
Britta Bensmann

Weitere Bestandteile des Lehrwerks
- *Schulbuch* (print und als E-Book)
- *E-Books* (in zwei Varianten: 1. alle *Topics in Context* bzw. 2. Schulbuch und *Topics in Context*)
- *Lehrkräftefassung des Schulbuchs* (im Unterrichtsmanager)
- *Handreichungen für den Unterricht* (print und im Unterrichtsmanager)
- *Workbook* (print)
- *Unterrichtsmanager*
- *Vorschläge zur Leistungsmessung* (digital)
- *Cornelsen Lernen App*

---

www.cornelsen.de

Die Webseiten Dritter, deren Internetadressen in diesem Lehrwerk angegeben sind, wurden vor Drucklegung sorgfältig geprüft. Der Verlag übernimmt keine Gewähr für die Aktualität und den Inhalt dieser Seiten oder solcher, die mit ihnen verlinkt sind.

1. Auflage, 1. Druck 2022

Alle Drucke dieser Auflage sind inhaltlich unverändert und können im Unterricht nebeneinander verwendet werden.

© 2022 Cornelsen Verlag GmbH, Berlin

Das Werk und seine Teile sind urheberrechtlich geschützt. Jede Nutzung in anderen als den gesetzlich zugelassenen Fällen bedarf der vorherigen schriftlichen Einwilligung des Verlages. Hinweis zu §§ 60 a, 60 b UrhG: Weder das Werk noch seine Teile dürfen ohne eine solche Einwilligung an Schulen oder in Unterrichts- und Lehrmedien (§ 60 b Abs. 3 UrhG) vervielfältigt, insbesondere kopiert oder eingescannt, verbreitet oder in ein Netzwerk eingestellt oder sonst öffentlich zugänglich gemacht oder wiedergegeben werden. Dies gilt auch für Intranets von Schulen.

Druck: H. Heenemann, Berlin

ISBN: 978-3-06-036526-5

PEFC zertifiziert
Dieses Produkt stammt aus nachhaltig bewirtschafteten Wäldern und kontrollierten Quellen.

www.pefc.de

PEFC/04-31-1156

Contents

Title	Topic	Text type / media	Skills	Page
Lead-in				6
Words in Context: English – a global language powerhouse	English as a world language The history of English	Informative text	Speaking	8
Info box: English: at home in many classrooms and countries			Speaking	9
Text 1: The future of English *Robin Lustig*	English varieties and threats to the dominance of English	Non-fiction text	Creative writing	10
Text 2: The influence of English on German *Matthias Heine*	Anglicisms in German	Newspaper article	Mediating	12
Text 3: Words and wordsmiths	How new words enter a language	Video	Viewing Speaking	14
Text 4: Culture clashes *Craig Storti*	Communicating across cultures	Non-fiction text	Intercultural communication Writing	15
Text 5: Do you speak bad English?	English as a world language	TED talk	Listening Intercultural communication	17
Text 6: Love speaks 'Reported missing' *Barry Cole* 'The quiet world' *Jeffrey McDaniel*	English as a language of poetry	Poem	Creative writing	18
Text 7: Art in Context: 'Girl on swing' *Banksy*	Playing with language	Graffito	Analysing visuals	20
Text 8: Navigating two cultures *Yasmine Gooneratne*	Language and identity Language and culture	Novel extract	Intercultural communication	21
Chapter Task: Communicating in English in everyday situations	Everyday English		Speaking	24
Support and Partner B				26
Acknowledgements				28

Abbreviations and labels used in *Context*

AE/BE	American English / British English
ca. *(Latin)*	circa = about, approximately
cf.	confer (compare), see
derog	derogatory *(abfällig, geringschätzig)*
e.g. *(Latin)*	exempli gratia = for example
esp.	especially
et al. *(Latin)*	et alii = and other people/things
etc. *(Latin)*	et cetera = and so on
f./ff.	and the following page(s)/line(s)
fml	formal English
i.e. *(Latin)*	id est = that is, in other words
infml	informal English
jdm./jdn.	*jemandem/jemanden*
l./ll.	line/lines
n	noun
pt(s)	point(s)
p./pp.	page/pages
pl	plural
sb./sth.	somebody/something
sin	singular
sl	slang
usu.	usually
v	verb
vs.	*(Latin)* versus *(gegen, im Gegensatz zu)*

🗺️	marks tasks that refer you back to the chapter's guiding question
Challenge	marks a more difficult task
▶ **Support**	refers you to the Support and Partner B pages (p. 26f.) where you can find more help to do the assignment
You choose	lets you decide which of the two given assignments you'd like to do
Intercultural communication	marks a task that focuses on intercultural communication
*****metaphor**	indicates that a word or expression (here: *metaphor*) is explained in the Glossary in the Student's book *Context*, p. 334ff.
▶ **SF 48: Paraphrasing**	directs you to the Skills File in the Student's book *Context*, p. 264ff. (here: Skill p. 9)
🔊	indicates that the sound file can be found in the Cornelsen Lernen App, eBook and UMA
▶️	indicates that the video can be found in the Cornelsen Lernen App, eBook and UMA
▶ **More info**	indicates that additional information can be found in the Cornelsen Lernen App
▶ **More language**	indicates that tips or further information regarding language can be found in the Cornelsen Lernen App
▶ **Check**	indicates that solutions to tasks can be found in the Cornelsen Lernen App
▶ **Getting started**	indicates that tips or ideas to get started on tasks can be found in the Cornelsen Lernen App

Speaking of English

1. **a** Look at the words in the illustration above. How have the words themselves and their shapes been formed? Examine the connection between meaning and form.
   b Some words are an example of blending (*spoon* + *fork* = *spork*). Think of other examples of blending.
   c Choose a word you like and create a word art image for it.

2. **a** Line up in order of how strongly you agree or disagree with the following statements. The left end of the line marks 'strongly agree', the right one 'strongly disagree'.
   1 English is easy.
   2 It's good that you can use English around the world.
   3 I like watching movies in the original English version.
   b Discuss your viewpoints.

3. Look at the Chapter map and speculate about the topics and the guiding question. Choose one item and brainstorm ideas. Exchange your ideas with a partner.

▶ More info

> **Chapter map**

What are the challenges of communicating in English?

Words in Context

▶ More language

🔊 English – a global language powerhouse

The history of English

English has been influenced by numerous factors that contributed to its evolution. Beginning with the Roman conquest of Britain in 43 AD, English has absorbed words from over 350 languages. Its total number of words is estimated at one million com-
5 pared to German with 400,000 or French with 100,000. Several thousand words were borrowed from Germanic tribes and the Vikings. Tens of thousands of French words entered English after the Norman invasion in 1066 had brought a French-speaking duke to the English throne who made French the official court language. Other important influences which shaped the way English is spoken today were the roughly 2,000
10 words William Shakespeare coined for his theatre plays and those added by the newly translated King James Bible of 1611. Regional accents, jargons and other varieties spoken by particular social classes have contributed to even more diversity. English expanded further with new words used by speakers in England's overseas settlements like America and Australia or countries under colonial rule in Africa and Asia who
15 needed to describe their surroundings. Not surprisingly, the spread of the British Empire until 1914 brought English to about 400 million people and caused new varieties to develop worldwide, like Jamaican English. Another variety is Chinglish (Chinese + English). This multicultural dimension makes English truly unique.

▶ More info

The importance of English

20 Today, English is the global language of politics, business, science, technology and travel spoken by a quarter of the world's population. It is also the official language in more than 50 countries. In others, like India, where no single national language exists, English serves the function of a *lingua franca*, a second language to facilitate communication. Some English variants, e.g. Pidgin English of West Africa, are simplified ver-
25 sions with combined elements of different languages. Non-native speakers of English actually outnumber native speakers by 3 to 1 and English has become the most popular second language globally. As English has achieved its status due to the political and economic impact and cultural influence of the nations where it is spoken, there are also fears that these nations may gain too much power.

30 ### The future

English has taken root worldwide despite its complexity and huge vocabulary: The spoken words often sound unlike their written forms and English spelling is complicated. An effort to simplify international communication by using an easy English version called Globish for busi-
35 ness and trade has not been overly successful. When asked about the future of English, experts suggest that more varieties of English will evolve and
40 that people will speak three versions of English: their home dialect, a national standard for work and school and an international standard English with a basic vo-
45 cabulary and simpler grammar which foreigners can understand.

Words in Context

1 Words words words

a Find three phrases in the text that are new to you, two that you find interesting and one that you want to add to your English vocabulary.

b Explain the phrases from **a** in English. Use a dictionary if necessary.

c In a group, present an explanation of your phrases. The others need to guess which one you are referring to. Take turns. Add at least one phrase and its explanation from your partners to your list.

d Start a mind map with words and phrases about English as a global language. Add to it while working on this chapter.

▶ SF 8: Working with a dictionary, Student's book p. 273

2 Language varieties

a Name three countries or regions whose languages have influenced the English language and summarize the reasons for this.

b Name at least four countries or regions where varieties of English are spoken today. Outline reasons for the emergence of these varieties.

3 Chunk it!

a Find suitable verbs for the blanks to form *chunks. You can check in the text for help but also add other verbs. If you are not sure, use a dictionary.

1 ... words from over 350 languages
2 ... new varieties to develop
3 ... native speakers
4 ... the function
5 ... a status
6 ... international communication

▶ Getting started
▶ Check

b Compare your chunks with a partner and add new ones to your list.

4 Globalspeak and new Englishes

You choose | Speaking | Work on task **a** or **b**.

a Discuss other dangers (cf. ll. 27–29) posed by powerful global languages you can think of and prepare a short speech.

b Do some research on Chinglish, Hinglish, Spanglish and Jamaican English and give a two-minute presentation to the class.

▶ SF 13: Doing research, Student's book p. 278
▶ SF 42: Preparing and giving a speech, Student's book p. 324

Info

English — at home in many classrooms and countries

As one of the most important global languages, English is taught at school, in universities or is studied privately by millions of learners worldwide. In Britain, English as a school subject for non-native speakers is called EAL (English as an Additional Language). In countries like France or Germany where English does not have an institutional role, English is taught as a foreign language (EFL). Where English does have an institutional role, such as in Nigeria or India, it is taught as a second language (ESL). English often functions as a lingua franca when it is used by people who don't share a common language (e.g. Germans and Norwegians talking in English on a campsite in Italy or in countries with more than one official languages not spoken by all citizens).

Whenever English is used alongside other languages in a country, a new variety of English may emerge with grammar and/or vocabulary that is influenced by the other language(s). One example of this is Singlish, an English variety spoken in Singapore.

1 Have **you used English as a lingua franca?** Talk about your experiences with a partner.

Text 1

The future of English Robin Lustig

- Find three reasons for learning English in the future. Exchange them with a partner and agree on the two most convincing ones.

You are going to read an article on English, its varieties and the influence technology might have on the relevance of the English language.

English is spoken by hundreds of millions of people worldwide, but do the development of translation technology and 'hybrid' languages threaten its status?

Which country boasts the most English speakers, or people learning to speak English?

5 The answer is China.

According to a study published by Cambridge University Press, up to 350 million people there have at least some knowledge of English – and at least another 100 million in India.

There are probably more people in China who speak English as a second language
10 than there are Americans who speak it as their first. (A fifth of Americans speak a language other than English in their own homes.)

But for how much longer will English qualify as the 'world's favourite language'? The World Economic Forum estimates about 1.5 billion people around the world speak it – but fewer than 400 million have it as their first language.

15 Of course, there is more than one English, even in England. In the historic port city of Portsmouth, for example, the regional dialect – Pompey – is still very much in use, despite the challenges from new forms of online English and American English.

English is the world's favourite lingua franca – the language people are most likely
20 to turn to when they don't share a first language. Imagine, for example, a Chinese speaker who speaks no French in conversation with a French speaker who speaks no Chinese. The chances are that they would use English.

Five years ago, perhaps. But not any more. Thanks to advances in computer translation and voice-recognition technology, they can each speak their own language,
25 and hear what their interlocutor is saying, machine-translated in real time.

So English's days as the world's top global language may be numbered. To put it at its most dramatic: the computers are coming, and they are winning.

You are probably reading this in English, the language in which I wrote it. But with a couple of clicks on your computer, or taps on your tablet, you could just as easily
30 be reading it in German or Japanese. So why bother to learn English if computers can now do all the hard work for you?

At present, if you want to do business internationally, or play the latest video games, or listen to the latest popular music, you're going to have a difficult time if you don't speak any English. But things are changing fast.

35 In California, Wonkyum Lee, a South Korean computer scientist for Gridspace, is helping to develop translation and voice-recognition technology that will be so

---

Annotations

3 **boast sth.** have sth. that is impressive
13 **World Economic Forum** Weltwirtschaftsforum
25 **interlocutor** person having a conversation with you
35 **Gridspace** company selling speech processing software

good that when you call a customer service helpline, you won't know whether you're talking to a human or a computer.

Christopher Manning, professor of machine learning, linguistics and computer science at Stanford University, insists there is no reason why, in the very near future, computer translation technology can't be as good as, or better than, human translators.

But this is not the only challenge English is facing. Because so many people speak it as their second or third language, hybrid forms are spreading, combining elements of 'standard' English with vernacular languages. In India alone, you can find Hinglish (Hindi-English), Benglish (Bengali-English) and Tanglish (Tamil-English).

In the US, many Hispanic Americans, with their roots in Central and South America, speak Spanglish, combining elements from English and the language of their parents and grandparents.

Language is more than a means of communication. It is also an expression of identity – telling us something about a person's sense of who they are. The San Francisco poet Josiah Luis Alderete, who writes in Spanglish, calls it the 'language of resistance', a way for Hispanic Americans to hold on to – and express pride in – their heritage, even if they were born and brought up in the US.

English owes its global dominance to being the language of what until recently were two of the world's most powerful nations: the US and the UK. But now, especially with the rise of China as an economic superpower, the language is being challenged.

If you are an ambitious young jobseeker in sub-Saharan Africa, you might be better off learning Mandarin Chinese and looking for work in China than relying on your school-level English and hoping for a job in the US or UK.

In the US itself, learning Chinese is becoming increasingly popular. In 2015, it was reported that the number of school students studying the language had doubled in two years and, at college level, there had been a 50% rise over the past decade.

In Uganda, however, all secondary schools must conduct classes entirely in English, and some parents teach their young children English as their first language. In many parts of the world, English is still regarded as a passport to success.

So is the future of English at risk? I don't think so, although its global dominance may well diminish over the coming decades. Like all languages, it is constantly changing and adapting to new needs. Until recently, 'text' and 'friend' were simple nouns. Now, they are also verbs, as in 'I'll text you,' or 'Why don't you friend me?'

Computerised translation technology, the spread of hybrid languages, the rise of China – all pose real challenges. But I continue to count myself immensely fortunate to have been born in a country where I can cherish and call my own the language of Chaucer, Shakespeare, Milton and Dickens, even though the language I call English is very different from theirs.

From: Can English remain the 'world's favourite language'?, bbc.com, 2018

Annotations
39 **linguistics** scientific study of languages
45 **vernacular** *(adj)* (here) local
55 **heritage** a person's ethnic, cultural or religious background
72 **diminish** become less important

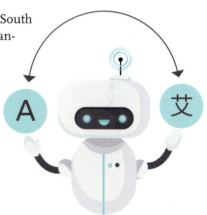

Text 1/2

Comprehension

1. Divide Robin Lustig's article into thematic units and condense them into a string of tweets (280 characters max. each).

Analysis

2. Analyse how Lustig conveys his attitude towards possible changes to his mother tongue and examine which effect this may have on the reader.

Language awareness

▶ More language

3. Lustig gives examples of conversion, i.e. using a word e.g. as verb, noun or adjective without changing its spelling (cf. l. 73f.). Other examples for this are: *eye, fool, host, cover, green, rise, cold*. Choose three of these words and write two sentences with each using them as different word types.

▶ Getting started

4. a Create a mind map for the concept of 'heritage' (l. 55). Add one branch for languages.
   b Speaking Prepare a one-minute talk about what your heritage and the languages you speak mean to you.

Beyond the text

5. *Quick write:* Why do machines fail to reproduce specific uses of language? Refer to what is said about computer translation technology in the text and reflect on what this means for this chapter's guiding question.

▶ Support p. 26

6. Writing Work on task **a** or **b**.
   a Rewrite the article in the typical tabloid newspaper style with catchy titles, lots of suggestive adjectives and comments on the different 'threats' to the English language.
   b Challenge Rewrite the article in the typical tabloid newspaper style with catchy titles, lots of suggestive adjectives and comments on the different 'threats' to the English language. Reflect on how this changes the message of the text.

Text 2

The influence of English on German   Matthias Heine

- Discuss reasons why German speakers might want to use words loaned from other languages rather than their own.

You are going to read an excerpt from an article by Matthias Heine in which he reports on different views about English loanwords, or anglicisms, in German.

Viele Menschen regen sich über Anglizismen auf. Jetzt sogar schon ein in Berlin lebender Engländer. Aber wie viele englische Wörter benutzen wir tatsächlich? Erstmals gibt es jetzt verlässliche Zahlen.

Mit seiner Aktion „Deutsch retten" und der zugehörigen Webseite hat der Brite Adam Fletcher wieder einmal gezeigt: Nichts regt Liebhaber der Muttersprache und erst recht „Sprachklugscheißer" (Fletcher) mehr auf als die anscheinend unaufhaltsame Flut von englischen Wörtern, die ins Deutsche schwappt. Allerdings zeigen die Eindeutschungen auf Fletchers Seite auch die Grenzen der Kritik an Anglizismen: Ein *Poster* ist nun mal im Deutschen nicht ganz dasselbe wie ein *Plakat* (so der Verdeutschungsvorschlag), und ob sich für den *One-Night-Stand* wirklich die Übersetzung *Einmaliges sexuelles Abenteuer* durchsetzen wird, mag bezweifelt werden.

Dennoch: Auch nicht zur Besserwisserei neigende Menschen finden, dass es zu viele Anglizismen gibt, dass sie häufig überflüssig sind und dass eine Häufung von englischen Ausdrücken Texte unverständlich und lächerlich macht. Der Sprachwissenschaftler Peter Eisenberg schreibt dazu: „Allerdings legt der Zeitgeist einen Missbrauch von Anglizismen besonders nahe, etwa wo einem prätentiösen Globalismus gehuldigt wird oder Texte gezielt unverständlich gemacht werden." Als besonders bedrohlich werden solche Angeberanglizismen empfunden, wenn Institutionen sie verwenden, denen Eisenberg eine „erhebliche Sprachmacht" nachsagt – wie etwa die Telekom oder die Bahn mit ihren berüchtigten Nonsensbildungen *City Call* und *Service Point*. [...]

Der Wissenschaftler Bernhard Kettemann ging 2004 von etwa 100.000 Fremdwörtern unter den ungefähr 400.000 deutschen Grundwörtern aus. Er schreibt: „Davon sind etwa die Hälfte im Duden Fremdwörterbuch verzeichnet. Nach meiner Schätzung sind etwa zehn Prozent Anglizismen, also etwa 5000 Wörter."

Eisenberg hat nun aus der umfangreichen Wortsammlung, die auch anderen Untersuchungen im „Ersten Bericht zur Lage der deutschen Sprache" zu Grunde liegt, zwei „Zeitscheiben" miteinander verglichen. Die eine Zeitscheibe umfasst die Jahre von 1905–1914, die andere die Jahre von 1995–2004. Eisenberg erläutert dieses Vorgehen: „Erfasst wird einerseits die Zeit zu Beginn des 20. Jahrhunderts, in der das Englische seinen Einfluss auf Kosten des Französischen ausbaut, und andererseits die Zeit am Übergang zum 21. Jahrhundert mit dem Englischen als dominanter Gebersprache für das Deutsche wie für viele andere Sprachen." [...]

In der ersten untersuchten Zeitscheibe von 1905–1914 sind unter 371.574 gezählten Wörtern 1299, die aus dem Englischen stammen. Ihr Anteil liegt bei 0,35 Prozent.

Um die Jahrtausendwende hat sich der Anteil deutlich erhöht: Unter den 381.191 wörterbuchfähigen Wörtern (die Wissenschaft nennt das *Lemmata*) finden sich 13.301 Anglizismen, das sind 3,5 Prozent.

Die Zahl entspricht auch dem, was für den Rechtschreibduden 1986 als Anteil genannt wurde. Dagegen hält Eisenberg die Schätzung auf Grundlage des Duden Fremdwörterbuchs für „viel zu niedrig". [...]

Text 2/3

50 Das Deutsche hat sich aber keineswegs als besonders anfällig für Anglizismen erwiesen. Häufig wird von „Sprachklugscheißern" ja behauptet, es gebe hierzulande eine besonders große Bereitschaft, englische Wörter zu übernehmen, weil man sich wegen der Nazizeit seiner eigenen Kultur und Sprache schäme. Das ist Quatsch: „Aller Wahrscheinlichkeit nach stellen die deutschen Anglizismen im
55 Vergleich zu denen anderer europäischer Sprachen keinen Sonderfall dar," schreibt Eisenberg nach Sichtung aller von Wissenschaftlern gesammelten Fakten. Es gebe aber Sondersprachen (so genannte Varietäten) mit mehr und solche mit weniger Anglizismen. Man darf wohl davon ausgehen, dass der Anteil in der Jugendsprache und der Gruppensprache der Internetnutzer besonders hoch ist.

60 Eisenberg kommt zu einem beruhigenden Urteil: Auch wenn sich die Situation in den vergangenen 100 Jahren „quantitativ und qualitativ" entscheidend verändert habe, sei der „strukturelle" Einfluss der Anglizismen nur „marginal":

„Untergangsszenarien für und Abgesänge auf das Deutsche sind nicht nur fehl am Platz, sondern sie untergraben die Loyalität der Sprecher zu ihrer Sprache." Mit
65 anderen Worten: Wer den Einfluss der Anglizismen übertreibt, übt Verrat an der Muttersprache.

From: 'So viel Englisch steckt wirklich im Deutschen', www.welt.de, 21 May 2014

▶ Getting started

▶ SF 47: Mediating from German into English, Student's book p. 332

1 `Mediating` During your exchange year in the USA, you have come across a number of loanwords from German that are used in the U.S. Your teacher has asked you to prepare a presentation in English on anglicisms in German. For this you use Peter Eisenberg's findings and other ideas from Matthias Heine's article.

Text 3

▶ More info

Words and wordsmiths

In his video Marcel Danesi talks about the ways new words enter a language and how they evolve over time.

- Point out why German words might enter other languages.

Comprehension

1 `Listening` Watch Marcel Danesi's TED-Ed video called 'Where do new words come from?'. Work on the following tasks.
  1. Note down the different ways a word enters a language.
  2. State why some words are absorbed into the language while others are not included in the dictionary.
  3. Outline the creation and development of the word *meme*.
  4. Point out the different 'fates' of words.

Text 3/4

Beyond the text

2 `Speaking` Probably more than 7,000 languages are spoken in the world. On the other hand, we have universal languages like mathematics and computer languages. In two big groups, prepare a debate on the motion 'The world would be a better place if we all spoke the same language'.

▶ SF 45: Having a debate, Student's book p. 328

Text 4

Culture clashes Craig Storti

- Outline why verbal communication between people from different nations might go wrong.

You and your partner are going to read texts describing the ways in which people from different countries communicate and why this can sometimes lead to irritation.

Partner B: Go to p. 26, read the text and work on the tasks there.
Partner A: Read the text below and work on task **1–3**.

Americans and Germans

Compared to Germans, Americans are quite liberal, even indiscriminate, with their praise (a charge, in fact, which Germans often level against them). While Ger-
5 mans reserve compliments for exceptional achievements, Americans lavish them on the most ordinary accomplishments. A worker doesn't have to exceed or even meet expectations to be given a word of encouragement. On the contrary, Americans will compliment workers merely for making a good effort, whatever the result, or in some cases just for having a positive attitude! The role of praise in America, in short, is not
10 so much to recognize excellence as to provide reassurance and build confidence. To put it another way, Americans need encouragement in a way Germans do not. A

Annotations
3 **indiscriminate** careless, unsystematic
3 **charge** *(n)* accusation
4 **level sth. against sth./sb.** aim criticism against sth./sb.
5 **lavish** heap on, shower
6 **exceed** surpass
10 **provide** give, supply

What are the challenges of communicating in English? **15**

Text 4

Annotations
12 **disheartened** discouraged
13 **resentful** bitter
14 **insincere** dishonest
17 **snafu** *(n, slang)* situation in which nothing happens as planned
18 **vigilance** watchfulness, carefulness
19 **time sheet** *Arbeitszeitnachweis*
20 **sloppiness** carelessness
25 **threshold** level at which something starts to happen

German will continue to turn in his or her best with or without recognition, but Americans become disheartened and even resentful if they are not recognized. Not surprisingly, Germans find American compliments empty and insincere. [...]

15 The German attitude toward compliments, or any kind of encouragement for that matter, is in large part a function of their perfectionism. Germans are especially intolerant of inefficiency – errors, mistakes, or snafus – anything that suggests a lack of discipline or vigilance. An untidy workspace, for example, or a leaking tap in the cafeteria, or an improperly completed time sheet – all of these would be
20 noted and possibly even commented on. There is never an excuse for sloppiness, whether physical or mental. The Germans pride themselves on the efficiency of their systems – and, not surprisingly, they have systems for virtually everything. They spend more time on worker training than any country in Europe. Needless to say, in a country where people expect perfection more or less as a matter of course,
25 the threshold for handing out compliments will be rather high.

From: The Art of Doing Business across Cultures, *2017*

Comprehension

1 Summarize the main points of the text.

Analysis

2 Examine the way the author uses language to point out the differences between US-Americans and Germans.

Language awareness

3 a Collect words and phrases used in the text to praise outstanding workmanship.
  b Modify these expressions to describe an average performance. Find more words and phrases which could be used for praising a good performance.
  c Present your notes on tasks **1–3b** to your partner.
  d Ask your partner what could improve the interaction between people from Germany and America.

Beyond the text

▶ Getting started

4 `Intercultural communication` Imagine your German school is hosting a student event with participants from Great Britain and the USA. Work on task **a** or **b**, keeping in mind what you learnt from Storti's texts.
  a With your partner make a list of 10 dos and don'ts for the students' meetings to avoid intercultural misunderstanding.
  b `Challenge` With your partner agree on 10 dos and don'ts for the students' meetings to avoid intercultural misunderstanding and present them in a well-structured poster.

Do you speak bad English?

- How important is it to speak 'good' English – for you personally, in business contexts, when travelling ...?

Speech and communication specialist Heather Hansen teaches business clients in multinational companies to speak better English. In her TEDx Talk '2 billion voices: how to speak bad English perfectly', she discusses global English and what efforts could be made for better communication between native and non-native speakers of English.

Comprehension

1 **Listening** Listen to Heather Hansen's talk and decide which of the following statements best summarizes Hansen's opinion.
   1 Misunderstandings in global communication would decrease if non-native speakers worked on their language skills.
   2 Native speakers should reclaim ownership of the English language.
   3 In global communication, adaptability is more important than your accent.

▶ Getting started
▶ SF 38: Listening/Viewing for gist and detail, Student's book p. 314

2 **Listening** Listen to Hansen's talk a second time, then complete the following sentences.
   1 The number of people born into English is ... .
   2 In order to increase understanding we need to ... .
   3 It is thought that miscommunication happens because ... .
   4 Non-native speakers feel judged on how they speak English instead of ... .
   5 Heather Hansen thinks it is important for a speaker in global communication to ... .
   6 In her view, listeners should ... .

▶ Check

3 **You choose** Work on task **a** or **b**.
   a List Hansen's recommendations to English native speakers.
   b List the reasons why non-native speakers seek Hansen's support.
   c With a partner discuss what Hansen's ideas could mean for this chapter's guiding question.

Beyond the text

4 **Intercultural communication** Heather Hansen thinks that the 'bad English' of non-native speakers is perfect as long as they get their point across while communicating. Discuss to what extent you agree with this view.

Text 6

Love speaks

You are going to read two poems about people communicating with difficulty.

- Think of a book or a movie where miscommunication is used as a form of comedy. Exchange your ideas with a partner.

▶ More info

Annotations
- 6 **peculiarity** unusual feature
- 9 **distinctive scent** characteristic smell
- 13 **level** *(adj)* having the same height
- 17 **outside** *(adj)* (here) apart from
- 18 **imply sth.** suggest sth. without saying it directly

A Reported missing Barry Cole

Can you give me a precise description?
Said the policeman. Her lips, I told him,
Were soft. Could you give me, he said, pencil
Raised, a metaphor? Soft as an open mouth,
5 I said. Were there any noticeable
Peculiarities? he asked. Her hair hung
Heavily, I said. Any particular
Colour? he said. I told him I could recall
Little but its distinctive scent. What do
10 You mean, he asked, by distinctive? It had
The smell of woman's hair, I said. Where
Were you? he asked. Closer than I am to
Anyone at present, I said, level
With her mouth, level with her eyes. Her eyes?
15 He said, what about her eyes? There were two,
I said, both black. It has been established,
He said, that eyes cannot, outside common
Usage, be black; are you implying that
Violence was used? Only the gentle
20 Hammer blow of her kisses, the scent
Of her breath, the ... Quite, said the policeman,
Standing, but I regret that we know of
No one answering to that description.

From: addictedtopoems.wordpress.com, *2015*

Text 6

B The quiet world
Jeffrey McDaniel

In an effort to get people to look
into each other's eyes more,
and also to appease the mutes,
the government has decided
5   to allot each person exactly one hundred
and sixty-seven words, per day.
When the phone rings, I put it to my ear
without saying hello. In the restaurant
I point at chicken noodle soup.
10 I am adjusting well to the new way.
Late at night, I call my long-distance lover,
proudly say *I only used fifty-nine today.*
I saved the rest for you.
When she doesn't respond,
15 I know she's used up all her words,
so I slowly whisper *I love you*
thirty-two and a third times.
After that, we just sit on the line
and listen to each other breathe.

From: The Forgiveness Parade, *1998*

▶ More info

Annotations
3 **appease sb.** make sb. less angry by giving him what he demands
3 **mute** (n) (obsolete) person who is not able to speak
5 **allot sb. sth.** give sb. sth. as a share of what is available

---

Comprehension

1 a Sum up each poem in one sentence.
   b Poem **A**: Note down the details the policeman asks for and the man's description of the woman reported missing.
      Poem **B**: Divide the poem into three parts and find suitable headings.
   c State why communication fails in both poems.

Analysis

2 Draw a large Venn diagram. In the shared area in the middle write down what the poems have in common and in each separate area, jot down what is different.

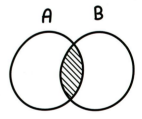

Language awareness

3 a Collect words, phrases and *metaphors the authors use to convey their love.
   b Describe the atmosphere their choice of words creates for the reader.
   c Choose one poem and replace all the words you found in **a** with sober, factual, less emotional words. How does the atmosphere of the poem change?

Beyond the text

4 **Writing** Work on task **a** or **b**.
   a Write what the long-distance lover in poem **B** is thinking while she is listening to her partner's I-love-yous.
   b **Challenge** Write in precisely 167 words what the long-distance lover in poem **B** is thinking while she is listening to her partner's I-love-yous.

▶ SF 36: Creative writing, Student's book p. 311

Text 7

▶ More info

Art in Context: 'Girl on swing' — Banksy

▶ Getting started

▶ SF 22: Analysing visuals, Student's book p. 292

Comprehension

1. Banksy's graffito appeared in a car park on Broadway in downtown Los Angeles, USA in 2010. Describe it and compare your notes with a partner.

   Language help
   show/depict sth. • body language • suggest sth. • spraying • whitewashing • bold lettering • capital letters • striking colour

Analysis

2. Analyse the graphical means used to portray the girl on the swing.

Language awareness

3. Examine the change to the word *parking* and describe the effect this might have on people who see the graffito.

4. Find other examples where small changes twist the original meaning of a word in a surprising way like Banksy does in his 'Girl on swing'.

Beyond the text

5. **You choose** Work on task **a** or **b**.
   a. Comment on the message of the graffito.
   b. Discuss whether graffiti appeal to you and whether you consider them an art form.

20 Speaking of English

Navigating two cultures   Yasmine Gooneratne

▶ More info

You are going to read an excerpt from a novel in which Navaranjini Mangala-Davasinha describes her and her husband Bharat's life in Australia, where they moved to from Sri Lanka in the early 1970s at a time when Australia experienced outspoken anti-immigrant sentiment.

How soon he had become unhappy! It occurred to me that he might be a good deal happier living in this foreign country if we both learned to speak the language. That very week, I went to the School of Languages at Southern Cross University, and asked if I could be enrolled as a student of Australian. But it didn't work out.
5 There were rows of Japanese students queueing up to learn English, and rows of Australian students queueing up to learn Japanese. Nobody seemed interested in teaching, or studying, Australian. I was very disappointed.

But I often have the radio on while I'm in the kitchen, and while I was listening to talk-back radio one day, I thought I would help my husband in a positive way by
10 improving my Australian vocabulary.

So I bought myself a notebook, placed it beside the radio in the kitchen, and whenever I heard an unfamiliar word, or heard someone say he represented seventy-five per cent or eighty-five per cent of all Australians, I jotted down whatever he had to say. That way I came across a lot of really interesting new words and phrases.

15 Some I found quite surprising. Like this very ancient Australian word which begins with a 'b' and rhymes with 'custard', which I first heard used – at a party! – by one of my husband's colleagues at the university. I consulted our host, who told me to my surprise that Australians use this word as a term of affection.

Professor Dory told me a story about an Australian academic he knew who had
20 apologised to an English don for using this word freely at a Cambridge sherry party. (Professor Dory is an Australian, of course, but he went to Yale for his PhD, my husband says, so he has to put on this really broad Aussie accent when he tells stories about Australians abroad.)

'Sorry, mate,' the Australian had said. 'I oughter've warned yer. Back in Oz, yer
25 know, we call everyone a bastard.'

The Englishman had gazed at him in mild astonishment. 'And why ever not?' he had asked.

Info

Racial laws
In 1973, the White Australia Policy was finally dismantled. It had forbidden the settlement of non-European people, especially those of Asian ethnic origin. These racial laws which were implemented in 1901, were gradually relaxed until Australia accepted migrants from any country of origin.

Annotations
9 **talk-back radio** programme inviting listeners to phone in and comment
13 **jot sth. down** write sth. down
16 **custard** [ˈkʌstəd] vanilla sauce
18 **affection** feeling of liking sb. very much
20 **don** teacher at a university
21 **PhD** = Doctor of Philosophy; university degree given to sb. who has done research in a particular subject
22 **broad** (here) strong

Australian and Sri Lankan flags

What are the challenges of communicating in English?

Text 8

Annotations

29 **linguist** professor of languages
30 **call sb. names** use offensive words about sb.
32 **genealogy** study of family history
38 **Woop-Woop** Australian for 'somewhere in the outback'
51 **G'day, darl** Australian informal for 'Good day, darling'
51 **come to terms with sth.** accept sth. by learning to deal with it
53 **distinct** clearly felt
56 **slit** *Schlitz*
57 **slope** *(v)* not going straight up
59 **time-honoured** respected because it has been done for a long time
60 **convict days** time when English prisoners were sent to Australia
60 **have a new vogue** come into fashion again
61 **anglicize sth.** make sth. English in character
63 **graduate** *(n)* person with a university degree

Professor Dory's stories were often about well-meaning Australians getting what he calls 'the warm sherry welcome' in Britain, and he's an expert linguist, my husband says, so I'm sure he's right in saying that Australians call people names when they really like them very much. He laughed heartily as he told me this story, so I laughed too. But I wasn't at all happy about it, not really. We Asians respect genealogy and well-established family lines and that word means … Well, there's just no way *I'd* have called anyone a bastard, however affectionate I might have been feeling at the time.

Except Ronald Blackstone. I'd have called *him* any number of good Australian names any time, with no affection at all in any of them. Ronald Blackstone is a sociology professor from the University of Woop-Woop who started up all our problems when he nicknamed a Sydney suburb 'Vietnamatta' because it was full, so he said, of Asians. (Far Easterners, he'd meant, of course.)

'Asians', he'd said on radio, 'pollute the air with the fumes of roasting meat. And we Australians,' he'd added, 'must be alert to the dangers involved for our society if we allow Asians in who cannot assimilate and accept our customs.'

Well, for weeks afterwards, the newspapers printed letters praising Professor Blackstone for speaking out on Australia's immigration policy. That was when my husband started having problems with his image, and I started listening carefully to talk-back radio, and watching television, and working hard on my Australian vocabulary. My notebook, which was filling up with new phrases on a range of different topics, gave me confidence. Whenever I got my husband alone, I tried out my new vocabulary on him. I felt this would give him confidence too.

One day, as he came in the door, I said, 'G'day, darl. I've come to terms with my sexuality.'

He looked alarmed to hear this, and I had the distinct impression that he avoided me for the rest of the evening. So the following day, I tried again with some new words and phrases I'd heard on talk-back radio that morning.

'Why should you care what Blackstone says?' I asked. 'Your eyes aren't slits and your head doesn't slope. It's obvious he doesn't mean *you*.'

My husband just looked depressed. 'Want to bet?'

Seeking ways to assimilate, we discovered the time-honoured Australian custom of name-swapping. Professor Dory says it dates back to convict days, and had a new vogue after war was declared in 1939 and hundreds of German immigrants anglicised their names practically overnight in Australia. And though there's no war on that I know anything about, it seems the grandfather of one of my husband's graduate students found that his family name of Michalakis was bad for business, so he swapped his name for a Scottish one. For two generations now they've belonged to the Australian branch of the Clan Mackenzie.

From: A Change of Skies, *1991*

Comprehension

▶ Getting started

1 Summarize Navaranjini's and Bharat's efforts to assimilate into Australian society and the disappointments they experience along the way.

Analysis

2 **You choose** Work on task **a** or **b**.
  a Analyse how the author achieves a humorous effect in this text.
  b Examine the means the author uses to characterize Navaranjini and point out what effect the choice of narrative perspective has on the reader.

Language awareness

3 **Intercultural communication** Examine the effect the term 'bastard' has on non-Australians as described in the text. Explain why swearwords, despite their common use in e.g. British or U.S. films, can cause intercultural offence if German students use them freely in Great Britain, Canada or the USA.

Beyond the text

4 Discuss Navaranjini's choices to improve her Australian English and suggest other methods she could have used to adopt new words or expressions.

5 **Speaking** Navaranjini and Bharat finally change their names to Jean and Barry Mundy in order to assimilate into Australian society. Work on task **a** or **b**.
  a In teams discuss possible effects of this decision on the Mundy's cultural identity.
  b **Challenge** You and your partner disagree about migrants changing their names to be accepted more easily in their new culture. Each of you list your arguments (for or against). Then act out the dialogue in front of the class.

▶ Getting started

Celebrating Australia's diverse people on Australia Day

What are the challenges of communicating in English?

Chapter task

Communicating in English in everyday situations

You have been accepted as a student volunteer in Britain. After you arrived in Britain, you find yourself in different situations where your communication skills are needed and tested.

1 It's your first day in Britain. In your introductory workshop you were given the information in the info box and a list of softeners, phrases to make the way you express yourself less forceful. A British volunteer takes you to your lodgings.

> **Info**
>
> **Not polite enough**
> Germans are often thought to be too direct, especially when speaking to people from the UK. For example, they do not say *please, thank you* and *excuse me* often enough.

a You have a couple of questions which you want to ask.
1 Where's my room?
2 Where do I meet the other participants?
3 When is the first meeting?
4 How many hours do I have to work per day?
5 Where is the nearest cashpoint?

> **Language help**
>
> Excuse me • Do you mind if ... ? • Could you/I perhaps ... ? • I was wondering if ... • Is there a chance that ... ? • Would you mind telling me ... ? • If it's not any trouble ... • Is it okay if ... ?

b Come up with five more sentences you might need at your new workplace which do not come across as too abrupt.

2 You see the other volunteers at an initial meeting. Before the official start, everybody is waiting quietly in the lobby. To avoid awkward moments when meeting strangers, it is a good idea to have in mind topics to talk about which people usually find interesting.

a Work with two partners. One of you picks a topic from the list of ice breakers on the opposite page and talks about it for two minutes without being interrupted. Afterwards the other two ask questions and share their views on the subject.

b Take turns.

Ice breakers
1. your favourite film, story or novel
2. your top five favourite foods
3. the most creepy villain from a film
4. a skill or talent you would like to have
5. your favourite kind of music
6. what you would take with you if you had to leave your house quickly
7. the animal you would like to be
8. the scariest thing you would like to do
9. a famous person you would like to meet
10. the era in history you would like to live in
11. five activities on your bucket list

3. At the start of the workshop each participant has a minute to briefly introduce themselves.   ▶ Check
   a. Prepare a powerful one-minute speech in which you talk about yourself, what motivates you to work for the organization you have chosen, what you hope to get out of this year in Britain and why you chose Britain for your year abroad.
   b. Give your speech in front of the other volunteers.

4. Two weeks into your stay in Britain you have got to know one another better and made some friends. Today, you and your friends plan to eat out at an Italian restaurant.
   a. Work with a partner. Decide who is the guest and who is the restaurant manager. You have to get the following points across over the phone:
      1. basic information (number of guests, the day and time when you wish to dine)
      2. particular table you would like to reserve which often tends to be booked already
      3. you want a good choice of vegetarian and vegan dishes
      4. you don't want the restaurant's three-course set menu but will choose one of the daily specials
   b. Take turns.

Language help
make a reservation • I do apologize • have a meal with friends • under what name • squeeze sb. in • what day were you thinking of • enjoy your meal • no problem at all • that's very good of you • a table by the window • I'm awfully sorry • please wait until you are seated

What are the challenges of communicating in English?

Support and Partner B

Text 1

▶ p. 12

The future of English

6 Support

You may consider the following aspects:

- Find an attention-grabbing headline with wordplay or emotive language, e.g. 'Is this the end of our language?'
- Sum up the article in one bullet point or as the first line of the article so that readers know what to expect.
- Write short paragraphs which are rarely longer than one sentence.
- Find snappy sub-headings in between to draw the reader's attention to the following paragraphs.
- Use quotes from Lustig's article to persuade the readers that a valid point is made.

Text 4

▶ p. 15

Annotations
2 **derive** come, originate
3 **implicit** suggested without being directly said
5 **squelch sth.** silence/crush sth. completely
6 **intimidate sb.** frighten sb.
6 **meekness** submission, resignation
7 **littered with sth.** containing a lot of sth. (maybe too much)
10 **subtlety** small but important aspect of sth.
11 **legacy** tradition, established practice
11 **stratified** divided into social groups or classes
12 **sufferance** tolerance
12 **better** (n) (here) Respektsperson
13 **circumspect** careful
15 **curb your tongue** control what you say
16 **mutton** Hammel
19 **beholden to sb.** owing sth. to sb.
19 **subservient** too willing to obey sb.

Culture clashes

Partner B

English and Americans

The English habit of understatement derives in large part from the great English instinct for fairness, here in the form of implicitly acknowledging the right of everyone to their opinion and to make it known to others. But to insist or otherwise
5 be too forceful in one's statements could be taken for trying to squelch other views or intimidating others into meekness. You will notice, in this regard, how English conversation is littered with expressions that acknowledge the other person's point without quite agreeing. 'I take your meaning, but …' 'That's well said, but …' 'I can agree with you – up to a point.'

10 Another part of the explanation for English subtlety (as Americans would call it) surely lies in the legacy of feudalism. In highly stratified societies, survival depended in large part on the continued good will and sufferance of one's betters. In such circumstances, people quickly learn to be circumspect in their speech, to say what they think other people want to hear, and […] to find ways to avoid saying what
15 others might object to. If curbing your tongue keeps a roof over your head and mutton in the stewpot, then you learn the art of understatement.

For their part, Americans associate plain speaking with liberty, and being unafraid to say what to think is perhaps the ultimate expression of individual freedom. It is, moreover, a symbol of equality, that no one is beholden or subservient to anyone
20 else. […] American directness may also be related to the fact that there was so much opportunity in the New World. What did it matter if you spoke your mind and caused offense? You could always move somewhere else and start your life over.

From: The Art of Doing Business across Cultures, *2017*

Speaking of English

Support and Partner B

Comprehension

1 Summarize the main points of the text.

Analysis

2 Examine the way the author uses language to point out the differences between the English and US-Americans.

Language awareness

3 a Collect examples in the text that show how English people soften an argument. Come up with more examples.
  b Modify the expressions from **a** into direct, 'unsoftened' statements.
  c Present your notes on tasks **1**–**3b** to your partner.
  d Ask your partner what could improve the interaction between people from England and America.

*Now go back to p. 16 and work on task **4**.*

Acknowledgements

Cover
Shutterstock.com/Dmitriip

Photos
p. 6/7 (M) background: Shutterstock.com/jessicahyde, dream: Shutterstock.com/bc21, shark: Shutterstock.com/Marek Tr, meow: stock.adobe.com/worldofvector; **p. 8**: Shutterstock.com/BEST-BACKGROUNDS; **p. 11**: Shutterstock.com/Irina Usmanova; **p. 13**: Imago Stock & People GmbH/Rudolf Gigler; **p. 15** top: stock.adobe.com/artinspiring, bottom: stock.adobe.com/jozefmicic; **p. 17**: stock.adobe.com/pressmaster; **p. 18**: Shutterstock.com/Veronika Kovalenko; **p. 19** oben: stock.adobe.com/Aleksandr, unten: Shutterstock.com/Creative Stall; **p. 20**: mauritius images/alamy stock photo/Robert Landau; **p. 21**: stock.adobe.com/sezerozger; **p. 23**: mauritius images/alamy stock photo/Peter Mundy; **p. 24**: Shutterstock.com/Pranch; **p. 25**: Shutterstock.com/DavideAngelini

Texts
pp. 10-11: Lustig, Robin. "Can English remain the 'world's 'favorite' language?" https://www.bbc.com/news/world-44200901, BBC.com, 23.05.2018 © *BBC*; **pp. 12-14**: Heine, Matthias: „So viel Englisch steckt wirklich im Deutschen", https://www.welt.de/kultur/article128260705/So-viel-Englisch-steckt-wirklich-im-Deutschen.html, *WELT* 21.05.2014; **pp. 15-16**: Storti, Craig. *The Art of Doing Business across Cultures*. E-book ed., Boston, Intercultural Press, 2017; **p. 18**: Cole, Barry. "Reported Missing." *Poetry Lover*, WordPress, addictedtopoems.wordpress.com/2017/05/13/reported-missing-by-barry-cole/. Accessed 24 Sep. 2021; **p. 19**: McDaniel, Jeffrey. "The Quiet World." *The Forgiveness Parade*, Manic D Press, 1998; **pp. 21-22**: Gooneratne, Yasmine. *A Change of Skies*. Picador, 1991, pp. 120-122; **p. 26**: Storti, Craig. *The Art of Doing Business across Cultures*. E-book ed., Boston, Intercultural Press, 2017.

Topics in Context

Context

Glimpses of the English-Speaking World

Themenheft

Cornelsen

Context

Glimpses of the English-Speaking World

Im Auftrag des Verlages herausgegeben von
Dr. Annette Leithner-Brauns, Dresden

Erarbeitet von
Martina Baasner, Berlin; Irene Bartscherer, Bonn; Lisa Braun, Meppen; Dr. Sabine Buchholz, Hürth; Wiebke Bettina Dietrich, Göttingen; Sylvia Loh, Esslingen; Benjamin Lorenz, Bensheim; Dr. Paul Maloney, Hildesheim; Dr. Pascal Ohlmann, Tholey; Birgit Ohmsieder, Berlin; Dr. Andreas Sedlatschek, Esslingen; Veronika Walther, Rudolstadt

In Zusammenarbeit mit der Englischredaktion
Dr. Marion Kiffe (Koordinierende Redakteurin), Dr. Christiane Kallenbach (Projektleitung), Aryane Beaudoin, Dr. Jan Dreßler, Hartmut Tschepe, Dr. Christian von Raumer, Freya Wurm *unter Mitwirkung von* Janan Barksdale, Irja Fröhling, Katrin Gütermann, Anne Müller, Neil Porter, Evelyn Sternad, Mai Weber

Beratende Mitwirkung
Ramin Azadian, Berlin; Heiko Benzin, Neustrelitz; Sabine Otto, Halle (Saale)

Layoutkonzept
Klein & Halm, Berlin

Layout und technische Umsetzung
Straive
designcollective, Berlin

Umschlaggestaltung
Rosendahl, Berlin

Lizenzmanagement
Britta Bensmann

Weitere Bestandteile des Lehrwerks
- *Schulbuch* (print und als E-Book)
- *E-Books* (in zwei Varianten: 1. alle *Topics in Context* bzw. 2. Schulbuch und *Topics in Context*)
- *Lehrkräftefassung des Schulbuchs* (im Unterrichtsmanager)
- *Handreichungen für den Unterricht* (print und im Unterrichtsmanager)
- *Workbook* (print)
- *Unterrichtsmanager*
- *Vorschläge zur Leistungsmessung* (digital)
- *Cornelsen Lernen App*

---

www.cornelsen.de

Die Webseiten Dritter, deren Internetadressen in diesem Lehrwerk angegeben sind, wurden vor Drucklegung sorgfältig geprüft. Der Verlag übernimmt keine Gewähr für die Aktualität und den Inhalt dieser Seiten oder solcher, die mit ihnen verlinkt sind.

1. Auflage, 1. Druck 2022

Alle Drucke dieser Auflage sind inhaltlich unverändert und können im Unterricht nebeneinander verwendet werden.

© 2022 Cornelsen Verlag GmbH, Berlin

Das Werk und seine Teile sind urheberrechtlich geschützt. Jede Nutzung in anderen als den gesetzlich zugelassenen Fällen bedarf der vorherigen schriftlichen Einwilligung des Verlages. Hinweis zu §§ 60 a, 60 b UrhG: Weder das Werk noch seine Teile dürfen ohne eine solche Einwilligung an Schulen oder in Unterrichts- und Lehrmedien (§ 60 b Abs. 3 UrhG) vervielfältigt, insbesondere kopiert oder eingescannt, verbreitet oder in ein Netzwerk eingestellt oder sonst öffentlich zugänglich gemacht oder wiedergegeben werden. Dies gilt auch für Intranets von Schulen.

Druck: H. Heenemann, Berlin

ISBN 978-3-06-035793-2

PEFC zertifiziert
Dieses Produkt stammt aus nachhaltig bewirtschafteten Wäldern und kontrollierten Quellen.
www.pefc.de

Contents

Title	Topic	Text type / media	Skills	Page
Lead-in				4
Words in Context: Traces of British colonialism		Informative text		6
Text 1: Does Britain need a museum of colonialism? *Alison Flood*	Postcolonialism: between tradition and change	Newspaper article Video	Speaking Viewing	8
Info box: The British Empire		Informative text		10
Text 2: Germany's colonial legacy	Postcolonialism: Living together	Video	Viewing Intercultural communication	11
Info box: German colonialism		Informative text		11
Text 3: The Commonwealth – family or foe?	The Commonwealth: contemporary implications	Video	Viewing Analysing videos Writing	12
Info box: The Commonwealth		Informative text		12
Text 4: Welcome to Nigeria! **Art in Context**	Nigeria: an emerging post-colonial state Nigerian identity	Pictures Infographic Video	Viewing Analysing videos Intercultural communication	13
Text 5: My vision of Nigeria *Aisha Yesufu*	Reality of life vs. dream of life	Essay	Analysing non-fiction Speaking	14
Info box: Aisha Yesufu		Informative text		14
Text 6: Welcome to Singapore! 'Bumboat cruise on the Singapore River' *Miriam Wei Wei Lo*	Singapore: a multi-faceted city state	Poem	Intercultural communication Creative writing	17
Info box: Singapore		Informative text		17
Text 7: Smart Nation Singapur – die digitale Stadt *Christoph Hein*	Singapore: a modern post-colonial state	Newspaper article	Mediating	20
Text 8: Forty shades of green *Johnny Cash*	Images of Ireland	Song lyrics	Speaking	22
Info box: Irish protest songs		Informative text		24
Text 9: Democratic disruption *Bill Rolston*	Ireland: a divided nation	Online article	Analysing non-fiction Writing	24
Info box: Irish president Michael D. Higgins		Informative text		27
Chapter Task: A time capsule				27
Support and Partner B				28
Abbreviations				30
Acknowledgements				31

Glimpses of the English-Speaking World

woman wearing a cap like that worn by freed Roman slaves, which became a symbol of liberty during the French revolution

Britannia, *personification of Britain, modelled after a female Greco-Roman warrior

the Titan Atlas, from Greek mythology, carrying the world, wearing a sash reading 'human labour'

▶ Getting started

Annotations
box 3 **sash** long piece of cloth worn over one shoulder

▶ SF 22: Analysing visuals, Student's book p. 292

▶ More info

1 With a partner, recollect what you know about the British Empire.

2 Look at the map on the opposite page. Point out what it tells you about
   - the size and the infrastructure of the British Empire in 1886
   - Britain's view of itself as a colonial power and of the colonized people and territories.

   Pay special attention to the animals and to how the people are dressed.

3 British artist and illustrator Walter Crane, a passionate socialist, included several details in the map to express his political convictions. Study the enlarged details and explain his hidden messages.

4 In this chapter you will learn about three English-speaking countries that were once part of the British Empire: Nigeria, Singapore and Ireland. Study the Chapter map, then discuss how Britain and its former colonies might still be affected by their colonial past today.

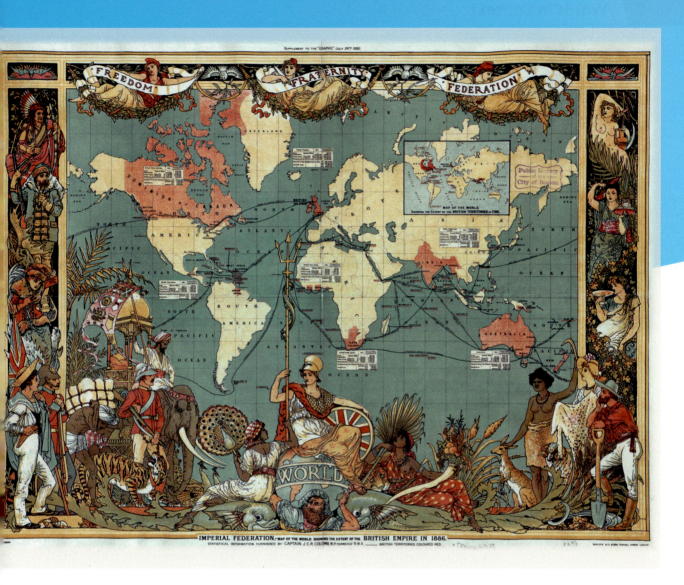

Chapter map

- impact of the colonial past on Nigeria, Singapore and Ireland
- postcolonial challenges
- Chapter task: a time capsule ✓
- Has Britain's colonial legacy been beneficial to its former colonies?
- legacy of Empire
- role of the Commonwealth
- burdens of colonialism

Words in Context

▶ More language

🔊 Traces of British colonialism

From Empire to independence

The British Empire has had a lasting impact on Britain and the territories it once ruled. At its height, at the beginning of the 20th century, the British Empire controlled one fourth of the land surface of the globe and was home to more than 400 million people.
5 In the decades that followed, many of them began to contest British domination and to push for independence and national sovereignty. For many territories, decolonization, i. e. gaining independence from British rule, was a long and demanding process. Colonial rule was exploitative and the newly independent countries had to deal with its consequences. In some of the new nations, the territorial boundaries and divide-
10 and-rule strategies that were a legacy of the colonial era led to ethnic conflicts, power struggles and sometimes even civil wars.

Glimpses of the English-speaking world: Nigeria, Singapore and Ireland

The differing colonial experiences and postcolonial settings impacted the process of nation building. While some countries saw the rise of authoritarian regimes and
15 dictatorships, others were more successful in defining their national identities and establishing stable political systems.
Nigeria, for example, which is Africa's most populous country, has been plagued by ethnic rivalries, patriarchal structures, poverty and corruption since it became independent in 1960, but it has also experienced an unprecedented economic boom
20 which has earned the country the nickname 'giant of Africa.'
Singapore, a comparatively small city state in South-East Asia, has developed into one of the wealthiest nations on earth since it gained independence in 1965. While Singapore has assumed global leadership in areas such as education and sustainable development, its government has also been criticized for being authoritarian and curtailing
25 citizens' freedoms.
Ireland was Britain's first colony in Europe. For centuries, the Irish resisted British oppression, and the oftentimes violent struggle for independence has left deep marks in the Irish national consciousness. After the Irish War of Independence (1919–1921), the island was divided, which has haunted Irish and British politics and societies ever
30 since.

The legacies of the Empire

Today most territories that were once governed by Britain are independent, yet they still show visible traces of British influence in language, politics and culture. The English language, for example, has become the world's lingua franca, not least be-
35 cause it was spread by British colonialism. Nowadays English holds official status in numerous postcolonial societies where it functions as the language of administration, parliament, the law, the media and also as the primary medium of education in schools and universities.
Several former colonies also adopted the British parliamentary system, and many
40 joined the Commonwealth of Nations, which was founded in 1931 to promote values such as democracy, justice, and peace and to foster cooperation in culture, sports and economy.
Despite these efforts, it must be acknowledged that imperial mindsets and racist attitudes going back to colonial times have prevailed in the UK to this day.

Words in Context

1 **Words words words**

   a Read the text and note down
   - two expressions related to the British Empire
   - two adjectives characterizing colonial rule
   - two expressions that describe the legacies of the British Empire
   - five expressions that reflect the main topics in the text.

   b Paraphrase the following expressions:
   British rule • decolonization • nation building • postcolonial settings.

   c Use the terms above to summarize the text.

2 **Clustering and brainstorming**

   a Cluster words and phrases from the text into the following groups:
   British Empire, decolonization, independence and *the legacies of Empire.*

   b Work with a partner and discuss which colonial legacies you consider positive and which ones negative. Together brainstorm more legacies of the Empire and add them to your cluster.

3 **Chunk it!**

   ▶ Getting started
   ▶ Check

   a Match the words on the left to those on the right to form meaningful *collocations.

   assume • curtail •
   establish • face •
   gain • leave •
   resist • populous •
   postcolonial • promote •
   show • push for •
   sustainable

   a stable political system •
   civil war • corruption • country •
   deep marks • development •
   ethnic conflicts • experience •
   freedom • leadership •
   independence •
   national identity •
   oppression • societies •
   values • visible traces

   b Choose either Nigeria, Singapore or Ireland and write five sentences about its development from colony to independent nation. Draw on your own knowledge or do some quick research. Use at least five collocations from **a**.

   c Compare sentences with a partner and add some of your partner's information to your sentences.

4 **Practice**

With a partner, discuss what aspects of the British legacy might be considered a benefit for its former colonies and which aspects a disadvantage? Write a short statement to be presented in class. Use words and phrases from the text and the exercises above.

Has Britain's colonial legacy been beneficial to its former colonies?

Text 1

Does Britain need a museum of colonialism? Alison Flood

In recent years, statues and other memorials commemorating slave traders and colonialists have been taken down or will be removed across the United Kingdom in response to campaigns calling for acknowledgement of Britain's colonial past and its role in the slave trade.

- Do you think it is a good idea to remove historical statues depicting controversial figures such as slave traders? What should the future of such statues be? Share your opinions in class, then read the article below that presents different opinions on the issue.

Britain should set up a 'museum of colonialism' where children will be able to learn about 'the really terrible things that happened in our past', the historian William Dalrymple has said.

Dalrymple, speaking in the final debate at the Jaipur literature festival (JLF) on
5 whether statues in Britain of former imperial heroes who would now be seen as war criminals should be placed in a museum of colonialism, or stay where they are, said that while he 'certainly wouldn't want to see most of the nation's statues torn down', people 'have to use discrimination'. The debate followed the toppling of the statue of the slaver Edward Colston in Bristol in June. [...]

10 'It's not a matter of being woke or a matter of being fashionable or trendy but it's being realistic about some of the really terrible things that happened in our past and teaching them to our children. If we put them in a museum of colonialism, this is an opportunity to teach, because we can set up a museum, which will do what at the moment what the curriculum fails to do.' [...]

15 Dalrymple said that the history curriculum for British school children sees them move 'from Henry VIII to Wilberforce and the impression they get is that the British empire was always about liberating slaves and always about anti-racism'.

'The things the British did in India and elsewhere are simply not taught in the syllabus and this is a problem,' Dalrymple said. 'When the British go out into the
20 world, they don't know what Indians know about the Raj or what the Irish know about the potato famine, they don't know what the Australians know about the mass extinction of the Indigenous Tasmanians, so we need to teach this in our schools and the opportunity of setting up a museum of colonialism with some of these war criminals and other statues seems to me an opportunity we must take.'

25 The historian Edward Chancellor, also speaking at JLF, disagreed. 'The current statue-bashing is part of the woke movement with its cancel culture, denunciations, forced confessions, censorship, intolerance and profound anti-intellectualism,' he said.

'Give an inch to these people and no statue will be left standing,' he continued. 'It
30 is an assault on the values of the Enlightenment and espouses a cultural nihilism. Behind this is a woke approach to history that is ill-informed, one-sided and anachronistic. It can't understand or accept that different periods have different values and that the historian should strive to be impartial.'

▶ More info

Annotations
08 **topple sth.** make sth. fall
10 **woke** aware of sensitive political issues such as racism or sexism
16 **Henry VIII** English monarch who ruled between 1509 and 1547
16 **Wilberforce** William Wilberforce (1759–1833), leader of the movement to abolish slave trade
20 **Raj** British colonial rule of the Indian subcontinent
30 **Enlightenment** philosophical movement in the 18th century emphasizing the importance of logic and science
30 **espouse sth.** support sth.
30 **nihilism** belief that all values have lost their meaning
31 **anachronistic** out of date

The journalist Swapan Dasgupta, who was also speaking in the debate, was similarly against removing statues. 'History was never going to be written on the basis of how one statue in Bristol looked,' he said. 'This is not an attempt to rewrite history or make history a little more even-handed. What it really amounts to is airbrushing history, throwing out a lot of unconformable things, and believing in sanitising the past to make it palpable to contemporary morality.'

Asked if statues in Britain should be removed to a museum of colonialism, 53% of the debate's audience said they should be, while 47% said they should not.

From: 'UK needs a museum of colonialism, says historian William Dalrymple'
theguardian.com, *16 September 2020*

Annotations
39 **palpable** that can be understood easily

Comprehension

1 What do Dalrymple, Chancellor and Dasgupta think about pulling down statues from colonial times? Summarize their opinions.

Analysis

2 The article uses several quotations. Explain their functions.

3 Assess which of the opinions you summarized in task **1** comes closest to your own views.

Language awareness

4 The adjective *woke* is a fairly recent addition to the English lexicon. It has become widely used, but is also controversial.

   a Use a monolingual online dictionary to trace original use and meaning of *woke*. Then compare this information to how *woke* is used in the article above (ll. 10, 26, 31). What differences can you detect?

   b Do an internet research to find out how the differences you observed in **a** came about and why many consider *woke* a problematic term today.

▶ SF 8: Working with dictionaries, Student's book p. 273

▶ SF 13: Doing research, Student's book p. 278

Statue of Edward Colston, Bristol, England, shortly before it was toppled

Has Britain's colonial legacy been beneficial to its former colonies?

Text 1

Beyond the text

5 The text alludes to several events in the history of the British Empire.

  a Collect the events mentioned in the text and put them in a chronological order.

  b Start a timeline of major events in the history of the British Empire based on your results from task **a** and on the information in the info box below.

> **Info**
>
> The **British Empire** was once the largest colonial empire in the world covering nearly one fourth of Earth's land area. Driven by its desire for raw materials and new markets, England started to establish trading outposts abroad as early as the 16th century. Over the next 300 years, more and
> 5 more territories would come under British domination as part of its bid to achieve economic and military superiority. The British Empire reached its peak by around 1920, when it ruled over approximately 20% of the world's population.
> In the aftermath of World War II (1939–1945), many colonies started to
> 10 seek autonomy and political independence. This led to a steady decline of the British Empire. Hong Kong was the last major colony to leave British rule when it was handed back to China in 1997, but Britain still controls some smaller territories around the world even though they aren't officially called colonies.

William Wilberforce

  c Work in groups of three. Each of you is assigned one topic on the British Empire:
    1 William Wilberforce (1759–1833) and the Slavery Abolition Act
    2 Black War (also known as Tasmanian War) (1824–1832)
    3 Irish Potato Famine (1845–1849)

Research your topic and prepare a three-minute talk. Focus on:
- essential information about the British Empire to be added to your timeline
- why your topic may or may not have been left out of the history curriculum for British school children.

▶ SF 13: Doing research, Student's book p. 278

▶ Check

  d [Speaking] Give your talks, then complete your timelines.

5 a Brainstorm reasons why the British Empire came to an end after 1945. Explain your ideas in class.

  b [Viewing] Watch a short video clip by the Imperial War Museum in London and check which of your ideas also feature in the clip. Add any new ideas to your notes.

▶ Support p. 28

  c In small groups, discuss what humankind could learn from Britain's colonial past to create a better future. Write a group statement and present it in class.

Glimpses of the English-Speaking World

Germany's colonial legacy

Before watching a report about the legacy of German colonialism in Namibia, do these tasks.

- ***Quick write:** Note down what you know about the history of German colonialism. Then share your knowledge in class.
- Read the Info box about German colonialism, then do the task.

> **Info**
>
> In the second half of the 19th century, Britain was not the only European power to seek **colonies overseas**. Numerous European countries, including the German Empire, were striving for the acquisition of colonial territories to create new markets for their products, gain access to valuable raw materials and pursue what
> 5 they thought to be 'civilizing missions' among people they considered backward. When thirteen European powers, together with the United States of America and the Ottoman Empire, met at a conference in Berlin between November 1884 and February 1885, the foundations were laid for the division between them of the African continent. The German Empire, which felt it had been lagging behind other
> 10 European powers, was allowed to occupy territories in West Africa (today's Togo and parts of Ghana and Cameroon), East Africa (today's Tanzania) and southern Africa (today's Namibia). Later on, in 1898, Germany also leased land in northeast China (around the city of Qingdao) and took possession of many islands in the Pacific. German colonial rulers did not refrain from exploiting and oppressing local
> 15 people to reach their goals. Among the most gruesome wars fought by the German Empire were the Herero and Nama Wars in present-day Namibia between 1904 and 1908, which ended in the killing of tens of thousands of Hereros and Namas – the first genocide of the 20th century.
>
> 1 Explain why the German Empire was eager to have colonies.

Comprehension

1. **a** [Listening] Work with a partner. While watching, partner A takes notes on the concerns of the Herero community, partner B on the German reactions to them. Compare and discuss your notes.
   b Watch the report again. Explain why Mr. Peringanda feels offended by the inscription on the war monument.

Beyond the text

2. [Intercultural communication] The report ends by saying that the wounds of German colonialism in Namibia have still not healed. In class, brainstorm ideas on what Germany and Namibia could do to help these wounds to heal.

▶ Support p. 28

Text 3

The Commonwealth – family or foe?

- Read the information about the Commonwealth.

Info

The **Commonwealth** is a voluntary association of 54 countries which work together closely to promote values such as democracy, human rights, education, equality, the rule of law, and peace. It was founded in 1949 by the United Kingdom and seven other independent nations which had formerly been
5 governed by Britain (Australia, Canada, India, New Zealand, Pakistan, South Africa, Sri Lanka). It was subsequently joined by many other countries, most of which had once been part of the British Empire. At present, there are 2.4 billion citizens living in the Commonwealth.

The Commonwealth Secretariat (founded in 1965) represents the interests of
10 member countries and provides support and assistance. It is managed by the Commonwealth Secretary-General, who ensures that the rules of the Commonwealth are followed. Every two years, the leaders of the member countries gather to discuss current global affairs and set their new priorities. The British sovereign has been granted the symbolic role of the head of the Commonwealth.

15 To promote unity, the Commonwealth works hard to bring its member countries together in many different ways, for example, through distance-learning programmes or sports events. Every four years, athletes from across the Commonwealth meet at the Commonwealth Games, the world's first fully inclusive sports event, to compete against each other and celebrate togetherness.

1 Describe the flag of the Commonwealth and try to explain what it symbolizes.

▶ More info

On Commonwealth Day the members of the Commonwealth commemorate their shared history and close ties. It usually takes place on the second Monday in March.

Comprehension

1 a Viewing Watch Prince Charles' message on Commonwealth Day 2021. Note down the topics he addresses in his *speech.
  b Viewing Watch the clip again and make notes on each topic.
  c Compare your notes with a partner. Together, write a statement in which you sum up the new goals of the Commonwealth envisioned by Prince Charles.

Annotations
'3"43 Terra Carta program started by Prince Charles to promote sustainable development

Analysis

2 The clip makes use of various film techniques. Analyse the functions of the long shots and medium shots used in the clip, of having Prince Charles speak directly to the camera, and of inserting film footage into the video.

▶ SF 39: Analysing films and videos, Student's book p. 315

Beyond the text

3 Writing The British writer and broadcaster Afua Hirsch has been highly critical of the Commonwealth, calling it *Empire 2.0*. Research Ms. Hirsch's arguments, then write a *comment on them.

▶ Check
▶ SF 26: Argumentative writing, Student's book p. 298

12 Glimpses of the English-Speaking World

Text 4

Welcome to Nigeria!

- **Partner B**: Look at the pictures on p. 28 and work on the tasks there.
- **Partner A:** Look at the pictures on the right.
- What aspects of Nigerian life are depicted? Which picture comes closer to your notion of Nigeria?
- Share your impressions with your partner and compare them. Together, study the facts in the box and relate them to your photos.
- In class, discuss which facets of Nigeria the photos and the facts do not reveal. *Cluster your unanswered questions on the board.

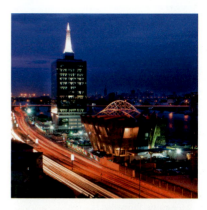

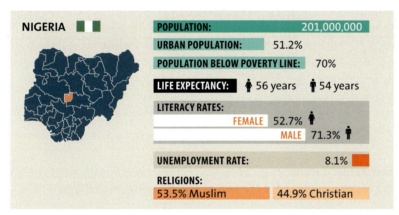

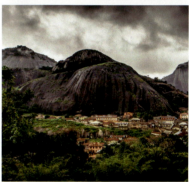

Data taken from: Henning Aubel et al. Der neue Kosmos Welt-Almanach & Atlas. *2020*

The clip you are about to watch may offer some surprising facts about Nigeria.

Comprehension

1. a **Listening** Watch the short clip twice and make notes on the following points: geography • people • religion • culture • economy.
   b Check whether the clip has been helpful in answering some of your questions about Nigeria.

Analysis

2. a Nigeria is often referred to as the 'giant of Africa'. Discuss whether the video supports or contradicts this *image.
   b **Viewing** Analyse what means the film uses to present this image of Nigeria.
   c **Intercultural communication** The video's presenter Leroy Kenton is Canadian. Discuss what consequences this may have for the presentation of Nigeria.

▶ Getting started

▶ SF 39: Analysing films and videos, Student's book p. 315

Beyond the text

3. **Art in Context** Visit Nigerian artist Ade Adekola's website and study his series *Icons as transplants* in which he explores the tension between local Nigerian identity and globalization. What new views of Nigeria can you detect? Discuss your ideas in small groups. Then choose your favourite artwork and present it in class.

4. Make your own collage about Nigeria entitled 'Nigeria – multiple perspectives.' You may use facts, images or quotes. Present your collages in a gallery walk.

▶ More info

Has Britain's colonial legacy been beneficial to its former colonies?

Text 5

My vision of Nigeria — Aisha Yesufu

- In 2020 Nigeria celebrated the 60th anniversary of its independence from British colonial rule. The picture shows the logo which was designed especially for that occasion. What could each element in the logo symbolize?

Annotations
2 **equity** fairness

Aisha Yesufu

Info

Aisha Yesufu (born 1973) is a prominent Nigerian political activist who has been fighting for justice and equity for many years. In 2014 she was one of the founders of the #BringbackOurGirls movement, which demanded the immediate release of more than 200 schoolgirls who had been kidnapped in northern Nigeria
5 by the Islamist terrorist group Boko Haram. Aisha Yesufu has also spoken out against police brutality in Nigeria. As a businesswoman and founder of the non-profit organization *Citizens Hub*, she promotes financial literacy to empower citizens to become financially independent.

The following text is Aisha Yesufu's contribution to a collection of essays entitled Remaking Nigeria, *published in the year of Nigeria's 60th anniversary.*

Annotations
05 **perish** die
06 **pale** *(v) (here)* seem less important compared to sth. else
07 **with impunity** without being punished
12 **abduct sb.** take sb. away by force
13 **rig sth.** manipulate sth.
13 **mar sth.** ruin sth.
14 **loot sth.** rob sth.
18 **docile** easy to control
20 **maim sb.** wound sb. causing permanent damage

I see myself someday sitting in a beautifully kept park in a bustling city in Nigeria with my grandchildren, telling them about the Nigeria that was. The Nigeria before they were born; the Nigeria that broke many and made many more lose hope; the Nigeria where young people mostly had one obsession: to leave the country even
5 though many perished trying to cross deserts and seas and some were sold into slavery. Those risks paled in comparison with little or no opportunities while at the mercy of trigger-happy security agents who killed young people with impunity.

I will tell them of the Nigeria where you had to know someone to become somebody and merit was sacrificed for connection; the Nigeria where access to good quality
10 education was dependent on the economic status of one's family. I will tell them of the killings and the lack of value placed on the life of a Nigerian and about girls who were abducted from their school just because they wanted to be educated. […]

I will tell them of elections rigged and marred by violence that brought in rulers whose main interest was serving themselves and looting public funds. I will tell
15 them of the time the Nigerian President spent months in another country for medical treatment and made Nigeria a laughingstock before the world; a country where the wealth of the nation was looted brazenly at the expense of national development. I will tell them of docile citizens who were too afraid to speak up and fight for a better nation for themselves. They prayed for things God had given them
20 capacity to do for themselves yet killed and maimed in the name of God. They fought for God and left their fight to God. I see myself telling them of the Nigeria where there was so much generational hatred amongst the citizens and people fought for tribal dominance and showed hatred to those not from their place; a nation yearning for identity; a nation which started with potentials for greatness
25 but failed to actualize those potentials.

My grandchildren will look at me and say, 'Stop kidding Grandma. That cannot be true!' [...]

I will look at my grandchildren and smile, knowing full well why they think that I am kidding them. How would they understand a period when many were ashamed to carry the Nigerian passport compared to when many would be doing everything they could to get the Nigerian passport and the opportunities that would come with being a Nigerian? By then, the improved quality of education and the literacy level of citizens would have led to an empowered and enlightened electorate who are able to make informed political decisions and choose candidates based on their competence, character and capacity and not based on their ethnicity, religion or gender. Our best and brightest would then be in leadership positions and not the worst of us as it used to be. Rigging of elections and political thuggery that once marred our elections would be distant memories; little wonder my grandchildren would be enjoying the dividends of democracy: good governance, accountability, and transparency. [...]

Equality and respect are two main factors that would have helped in building the Nigeria of my grandchildren. Gone would be the days when Nigerians fought over tribal and religious superiority. What will matter in the Nigeria of my grandchildren will be our identity as Nigerians and not our ethnic identities as Efik, Igbo, Yoruba, Hausa, Fulani, Ijaw, Ogoni, Tiv, Ebira, etc. Everyone will have the opportunity to key into the Nigerian dream without discrimination. Citizens will be accorded respect and dignity. The life of every Nigerian will be worthy of the attention of the state and will be protected at all costs. The Nigeria of my grandchildren will have citizens that will give their all to their country and will be ready to die for it. A country that dignifies you will have your loyalty.

Looking around in the park with my grandchildren, it will be hard to believe that Nigeria was once the poverty capital of the world, a country where unemployment was once so high and infrastructural development so minimal. How are my grandchildren to comprehend how citizens endured not having regular electricity or that there were children like them that roamed the streets, abandoned by their parents and that many who should have called for the system that kept them on the street to be abolished, supported it? Or that it was like a crime to be poor in Nigeria of the past and the only time that the poor mattered was during election where their thumbprints could be exploited for pittance. We would truly have come a long way as a nation; our perseverance led us this far. We would once again be the happiest people on earth. [...]

Many will say these are pipe dreams. As I look at the reality of Nigeria as we celebrate our 60th year of independence, a part of me wants to agree with them and just give up the fight for a new and better Nigeria. But then, there is a stronger part of me that sees the Nigeria of my grandchildren being a reality. Giving up on Nigeria is so easy; it means we do not have to do anything other than complain and keep looking for an opportunity to leave the country and go to countries that were once in the situation we are in today but had citizens who refused to give up and believed in having a functional and prosperous nation and worked hard to achieve it.

Looking at the great possibility of what Nigeria can be and believing in that possibility is a lot harder. It means we must do our bit to get the Nigeria that we deserve.

Annotations
33 **electorate** all people who are allowed to vote
37 **thuggery** brutal crime
47 **dignity** the fact of being given respect
59 **pittance** very small amount of money
60 **perseverance** [ˌpɜːsəˈvɪərəns] continued effort despite difficulties
62 **pipe dream** fantastic or unrealistic plan

Text 5

We must never set goals based on our present reality but based on what we want. A prosperous and great Nigeria is something that many of us want even when there are many who think it is not achievable. It is! The first and most important
75 step is to believe. Let us collectively do what we can to achieve this new Nigeria we yearn for. We can achieve that by working together rather than working against one another. In the words of Nelson Mandela, the first black president of South Africa, 'It always seems impossible, until it's done.'

I know that the Nigeria of today is not our destiny. There is a Nigeria for the unborn
80 generation that we should fight for just as others fought to make Nigeria independent sixty years ago. We cannot afford to give up on that Nigeria.

I know by the grace of God Almighty,

#NigeriaMustWorkInOurLifetime.

From: The Nigeria that I see, *in:* Remaking Nigeria. Sixty Years, Sixty Voices, 2020.

▶ SF 17: Reading and understanding non-fictional texts, Student's book p. 285

▶ Check

A protester during a demonstration against police brutality in Lagos, Nigeria

▶ Support p. 29

Comprehension

1 a Summarize the problems of contemporary Nigeria and the country's potential as Aisha Yesufu sees them.
  b Ms. Yesufu alludes to several events in modern Nigerian history. Match the events below to passages in her *essay and explain why she uses these historical allusions.
  - *Nigerian Civil War (1967–1970):* a war fought between the central government and the Republic of Biafra, which was set up by nationalists of the Igbo ethnic group in an attempt to declare independence from Nigeria
  - *Chibok schoolgirls kidnapping (2014):* abduction of more than 270 mostly Christian girls aged between 16 and 18 by the Islamist terrorist group Boko Haram
  - *Nigerian refugee crisis (since 2014):* displacement of 2.4 million people since Boko Haram's attacks started
  - *President Buhari's stay abroad (2017):* extended medical treatment of the Nigerian president in the UK, lasting for more than 100 days

Analysis

2 Ms. Yesufu emphasizes the importance of national identity for Nigeria's future while downplaying the importance of ethnic identity. Analyse how she does so and why.

> **Language help**
> personal pronoun • include/exclude sb. from ... • contrast sth. to • refer to sb. as ... • use proper names

16 Glimpses of the English-Speaking World

Text 5/6

Language awareness

3 a Ms. Yesufu uses the phrase 'I will tell them ...' repeatedly in her essay. Explain the intended effect. Then give more examples of *repetition and parallel structures in the essay.

b Write a short paragraph in which you imagine what you will tell your grandchildren about your home country in sixty years' time. Use repetition and parallel structures.

Beyond the text

4 a Note down the main features of Aisha Yesufu's Nigerian dream.

b [Challenge] [Speaking] Compare Aisha Yesufu's Nigerian Dream with the American Dream. Give a 2-minute talk about them.

Text 6

Welcome to Singapore!

- Singapore has several nicknames. Look at the two pictures and guess what the following nicknames could mean: *The Little Red Dot, The Garden City, The Lion City, The Asian Tiger, The Fine City*. Do an internet research of how Singapore got its nicknames and check whether your initial ideas were correct.

- Read the Info box about Singapore.

> **Info**
>
> The city state of **Singapore**, home to nearly 6 million citizens, is one of the most prosperous countries in the world. It consists of Singapore Island (Malay 'Pulau Ujong', meaning 'land's end') and more than 60 smaller islands in the Malayan archipelago. Legend has it that Singapore received its name from a Sumatran
> 5 prince who reigned over the region in the 14th century. While on a hunt the prince encountered a big animal, which his advisors believed to be a lion. This eventually led to renaming the region 'Singapura', meaning 'lion'. Ironically, the animal that the prince might have spotted was probably a Malayan tiger, as lions never lived in this part of the world.
> 10 Modern Singapore dates back to the early 19th century. In 1819, Sir Thomas Stamford Raffles, a British statesman, negotiated a treaty with local rulers that

Text 6

allowed the British to open a new trading port on the island, which was located at a strategically important position along the sea route between British India and China. The port developed quickly, drawing more and more immigrants from China, India and the Malayan archipelago to its shores. Half a decade later, in 1867, Singapore became a crown colony.

In World War I (1914–18) Singaporean life was not affected significantly, whereas in World War II (1939–45) it was impacted greatly. In the Battle of Singapore (February 1942), British forces were defeated by the Japanese Empire, which would occupy the territory for the following three years and rename it 'Syonan-to' ('light of the south' in Japanese). After the war, Singapore was returned to the British, who granted the people of Singapore more self-government when demands for self-rule became stronger. It was not before 1965, however, that Singapore finally became an independent republic.

The new Singaporean government, headed by Prime Minister Lee Kuan Yew, was highly successful at modernizing the country, which led to an unprecedented economic boom greatly admired by other postcolonial nations whose transition to independence proceeded less smoothly. By the 1990s, Singapore had become one of the world's richest nations. Today Singapore is praised for its political stability, its security, its education system, its economic competitiveness coupled with sustainable development – and its cleanliness! Critics, on the other hand, argue that Singapore is not truly democratic, pointing to the fact that Singapore has, since independence, been dominated by only one party, the People's Action Party (PAP), and accusing the government of neocolonial authoritarianism and repression of oppositional voices.

Singaporeans are proud of their multiethnic, multicultural and multireligious heritage, which is reflected in the city's architecture, art, food, and festivals. Ethnic Chinese comprise three-fourths of Singapore's total population today, with Malays and Indians coming second and third. Far from homogenous, each community speaks a wealth of different languages and dialects. The official languages of Singapore are Mandarin Chinese, Malay, Tamil, and English. As the language of the former colonizers, English is the main medium for administration and business and is also the preferred language of instruction in Singapore's schools and universities.

Info

Miriam Wei Wei Lo (born 1973) is an Australian poet who considers herself 'complicated'. Born in Canada to a Chinese-Malaysian father and an Anglo-Australian mother, she grew up in Singapore and then moved to Australia to study. Today she lives in Western Australia. She has published several collections of poetry and a children's book which reflect many aspects of her own cultural heritage and cross-cultural experiences.

1. Mention two aspects that surprised you, two that you already knew about Singapore and two that were new to you. Talk about your lists with a partner.

- Discuss whether Singapore's development could serve as a model for the future of other independent nations that were once part of the British Empire.

The poem 'Bumboat cruise on the Singapore River' by Miriam Wei Wei Lo on the next page takes readers on a cruise down Singapore River, a popular tourist attraction.

Glimpses of the English-Speaking World

Text 6

Bumboat cruise on the Singapore River   Miriam Wei Wei Lo

Rhetoric is what keeps this island afloat.
Singaporean voice with a strong American accent,
barely audible above the drone of the bumboat engine:
'Singaporeans are crazy about their food.
5 They are especially fond of all-you-can-eat buffets.
Why not do as the locals do and try out one of the buffets
at these hotels along the waterfront.' The Swissotel looms.
The Grand Copthorne. The Miramar. All glass
and upward-sweeping architecture. Why not do
10 as the locals do. Here in this city where conspicuous consumption
is an artform. Where white tourists wearing slippers and singlets
are tolerated in black-tie establishments. Dollars. Sense.

How did I ever live in this place? Sixteen years of my life
afloat in this sea of contradictions, of which I was, equally, one:
15 half-white, half-Chinese; the taxi-driver cannot decide
if I am a tourist or a local, so he pitches at my husband:
'Everything in Singapore is changing all the time.'
Strong gestures. Manic conviction. 'This is good.
We are never bored. Sometimes my customers
20 ask me to take them to a destination, but it is no longer there.'
We tighten our grip on two squirming children and pray
that the bumboat tour will exist. Nothing short of a miracle
this small wooden boat which is taking us now past Boat Quay,
in its current incarnation, past the Fullerton Hotel

25 To the mouth of the Singapore river, where the Merlion
still astonishes: grotesque and beautiful as a gargoyle.
The children begin to chafe at confinement. My daughter wails
above the drone of the engine. There's talk of closing the mouth
of the river. New water supply. There's talk of a casino.
30 Heated debate in the Cabinet. Old Lee and Young Lee
locked in some Oedipal battle. The swell is bigger out here
in the harbour, slapping up spray against the sides of the boat,
as if it were waves that kept it afloat, this boat,
this island, caught between sinking and swimming,
35 as I am caught now. As if rhetoric mattered.
As if this place gives me a name for myself.

From: Westerly, 2005

Annotations
10 **conspicuous** striking, easy to notice
11 **singlet** sleeveless undershirt
18 **manic** very excited
21 **squirm** move around uncomfortably or nervously
24 **incarnation** (here) state, condition
25 **Merlion** mythical creature that is half mermaid, half lion spouting water into the Singapore River; Singapore's mascot and one of its most famous landmarks
26 **gargoyle** ugly figure made of stone, usually spouting rainwater from a roof
27 **chafe at sth.** be annoyed and impatient about sth. because it limits you
30 **Old Lee** Lee Kuan Yew, Singapore's first Prime Minister up until 1995
30 **Young Lee** Lee Hsien Long, became Prime Minister in 2004
31 **Oedipal** [/ˈiːdɪpl/] (here) psychologically complex

Comprehension

1 Read the poem to find out ...
   - who is taking the bumboat cruise
   - what happens before the tour starts
   - which sights can be seen from the boat
   - what they learn about Singapore
   - what the boat ride makes the *speaker think of
   - how the boat ride makes the speaker feel.

   Quote lines from the poem.

▶ SF 19: Reading and understanding poetry, Student's book p. 287

▶ Check

Text 6/7

Analysis

2   a   The poem uses the word 'rhetoric' twice to describe contemporary Singapore and the Singaporean lifestyle (ll. 1, 35). Explain this lexical choice in the context of the poem.
    b   Analyse the *speaker's ambivalent relationship to Singapore. Take into account the following aspects: What ties the speaker to the country? What aspects does the speaker find perplexing? And how does this affect the speaker's sense of self?

Language awareness

▶ More language
▶ SF 36: Creative writing, Student's book p. 311

3   a   Explain the use of the present progressive 'is changing all the time' (l. 17).
    b   **Writing** Put yourself in the situation of the speaker on the bumboat and write a short *interior monologue. Use the present progressive with *all the time* or *always*.

Beyond the text

4   **You choose** Work on either of the tasks below.

▶ SF 36: Creative writing, Student's book p. 311
▶ SF 41: Giving a presentation, Student's book p. 321

a **Writing** Work with a partner. Imagine after a long day of sightseeing in Singapore the speaker calls a very good friend in Australia and talks about their day. Do some research, then write their *dialogue and act it out.

b **Intercultural communication** Singapore's cuisine is as diverse as its cultures. In small groups, prepare short presentations on popular, multicultural Singaporean dishes.

Text 7

Smart Nation Singapur – die digitale Stadt   Christoph Hein

- What is your vision of a 'smart nation' or 'smart city'? Brainstorm ideas.

Der strenge Stadtstaat vernetzt sich wie kein anderes Land der Erde. Schon heute geht fast alles mit dem Handy. Dazu braucht es visionäre Politiker – und folgsame Bürger.

Morgens gegen elf Uhr lässt Benedikt Tschörner Manila überfluten. „Andere
5   reden vom Anstieg des Meeresspiegels, wir zeigen ihn", sagt er. Dann schiebt Tschörner den Regler am linken Rand des riesigen Bildschirms noch höher, das digitale Stadtbild färbt sich blau und blauer. „Der Klimawandel wird dazu führen, dass große Stadtgebiete Manilas in 80 Jahren überflutet sein werden, wird nicht sehr schnell etwas getan", sagt der Entwickler des Fraunhofer Instituts in Singapur.
10 Die philippinische Hauptstadt gilt den Informatikern im Stadtstaat nur als Testobjekt ihrer Methoden. Eigentlich arbeiten sie am drohenden Überschwemmungs-Szenario Singapurs. Sehen dürfen das aber bislang nur Auserwählte. „Die Bevölkerung wird die Auswirkungen später in Simulationsräumen erleben können", sagt Tschörner. „Zunächst liefern wir den Entscheidern Grundlagen."
15 Virtuelle Stadtmodelle für die Modellstadt sind nur ein Hilfsmittel, das die Singapurer nutzen auf ihrem Weg, aus ihrer Smart City eine Smart Nation zu

machen. In der Tropenstadt ohne eigene Bodenschätze wird groß gedacht. Auch in Punggol. Fast 200 Jahre ist es her, da zogen die Malaien hier Fruchtbäume hoch. „Punggol", der Stadtteil im Nordosten Singapurs, steht für die Stecken, welche die Bäume damals beim Wachstum stützten. Heute lassen hier chinesische Baukonzerne immer mehr Hochhäuser für 160.000 Menschen heranwachsen. Zu ihren Füßen entsteht der Punggol Digital District: 50 Hektar, 28.000 Arbeitsplätze, 12.000 Studenten – ein Leitbild für die Smart Nation Singapur. [...]

Schon jetzt hat Singapur auf dem Weg zur Smart Nation viel erreicht, mehr als fast alle anderen Städte dieser Welt. Steuererklärung? Dauert hier nur zwanzig Minuten am Bildschirm, weil man nur Veränderungen gegenüber dem Vorjahr angeben muss. [...]

Für fast alles ist digital gesorgt. Eintrittskarte in die schöne neue Digitalwelt am Äquator ist der Sing-Pass. Wie das „Sesam öffne dich" bei Ali Baba und den 40 Räubern öffnet er die Tür zu den Ämtern des Staates – Klicks und Passwörter sind Vergangenheit. [...] Der SingPass aber bildet nur die Oberfläche, welche die Bürger direkt nutzen. Dahinter wächst in Hochgeschwindigkeit eine virtuelle Welt heran: Für Punggol, aber auch den kommenden Stadtteil Jurong Innovation District mit seinen 600 Hektar, nutzen die Entwickler immer häufiger „Digital Twins", virtuelle Zwillinge der Wirklichkeit. „Beim Bau von Fabriken unter dem Konzept Industrie 4.0 ist das ja üblich. Der Bau ganzer Stadtteile zunächst am Bildschirm ist dann aber noch mal viel komplizierter", sagt Wolfgang Müller-Wittig. Der Professor und Standortleiter des Ablegers der Deutschen Fraunhofer Gesellschaft im fünften Stock der Nanyang Technological University unterstützt Singapur seit 20 Jahren auf dessen Weg in die digitale Zukunft. [...]

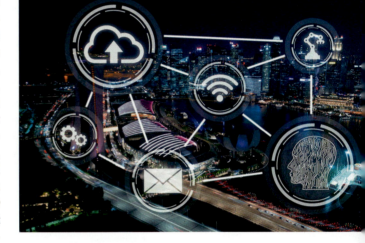

„Die Smart Nation hat so viele Aspekte", sagt Müller-Wittig. Wie auch Tan im JTC-Turm meint er: „Der Weg muss nun dahin führen, die Systeme immer weiter zusammenzubinden, und das mit so wenigen Daten wie nur möglich." Das Zusammenführen aber gilt nicht nur für Daten: „Singapur scannt die Welt und holt sich dann die besten Talente." [...]

Ist das Ziel zu erkennen, wissen Forscher und Manager indes, dass der Weg dorthin weit ist. Kein Bereich Singapurs bleibt unberührt. Das aber sorgt auch für Risiken. Sie scheinen nicht allen im Stadtstaat jederzeit bewusst, und die Deutungshoheit gibt, wie immer, die seit Staatsgründung 1965 amtierende Regierungspartei vor. Zehntausende zusätzliche Kameras zur Überwachung der kleinsten Regung der Bürger? Kein Problem, sichern sie ja unser aller Sicherheit. Die rasante Zunahme digitaler Diebstähle, bei denen Täter auch über Tage unbemerkt Tausende von Dollar von Privatkonten bei Asiens „bester digitaler Bank", der DBS Group, abräumen? Das ist schlecht, die Aufklärung dauert neun Monate, die Erstattung durch die Bank ist ungewiss – Singapur aber beginnt eine Kampagne, die vor Datendiebstahl warnt. [...]

Text 7/8

Wer glaubt, der Stadt ginge es bei all dem nur um bessere Dienstleistungen für ihre Bürger, kennt Singapur nicht. Die Digitalisierung wirft mindestens zwei Nebeneffekte ab: Der Stadtstaat gilt als eine der am besten überwachten Gesellschaften der Welt. Was aber in China anstößig wirkt, wird hier immer noch als hilfreich und schützend verstanden. Weniger umstritten ist der Abstrahleffekt auf das Ausland: Noch sind die übrigen neun südostasiatischen Länder in weiten Teilen unterentwickelt – Singapur ist den Nachbarländern meilenweit voraus. Wird die Digitalisierung gepaart mit Industrie 4.0, mit Robotik, mit Energie-, Medizin- oder Nahrungstechnik, wird immer öfter Künstliche Intelligenz zum Einsatz kommen, wachsen die Exportchancen. [...]

Läuft alles gut, dürfen sich Bosch in Stuttgart und der TÜV Süd im fernen München ein kleines Stück von der Zukunft Singapurs als Smart Nation abschneiden. Immer dann, wenn in einem Gebäude auf der Insel ein Aufzug herauf- oder herunterfährt, will ein Team der beiden die Daten erheben, um dank der Fernwartung drohende Ausfälle frühzeitig zu erkennen – bevor es zu einem Unfall kommen kann. [...]

„Hier in Singapur sind sie Deutschland um Meilen voraus. Ich wünschte mir, dass man sich dort ein Stück von Singapur abschnitte", sagt Tschörner, während er seinen Datenhelm im Fraunhofer Institut zur Seite legt. Er hält inne. „Die Regierung hier hat sich alle Mittel gesichert, mit denen sie theoretisch den übelsten Horrorstaat der Welt bauen könnte. Dieser Grad der Digitalisierung geht aus meiner Sicht überhaupt nur, weil die Regierung hier in Singapur so ordentlich arbeitet."

From: Frankfurter Allgemeine Zeitung, *31 May 2021*

▶ Getting started
▶ SF 47: Mediating written and oral texts, Student's book p. 332

1 Mediating Imagine you are an intern at Germany's Fraunhofer Institute in Singapore. Summarize for your Singaporean colleagues what the article says about how Singapore tries to improve the quality of life for its citizens and what Germany could learn from it.

Text 8

▶ More info

Info
Johnny Cash (1932–2003) was one of the most popular U.S. singer-songwriters in the history of American music. His music covers a wide range of *genres, including country, rock, and blues, which he mixed innovatively to create a unique hybrid sound.

Forty shades of green — Johnny Cash

- Finish this sentence in as many ways as possible: *When I think of Ireland I think of ...*
- Compare your ideas with at least three other classmates.
- In class, cluster your ideas about Ireland.

Glimpses of the English-Speaking World

Text 8

In 1959 Johnny Cash wrote the song 'Forty shades of green' while on a trip to Ireland. The song has become a classic both in the U.S. and in Ireland.

I close my eyes and picture the emerald of the sea
From the fishing boats at Dingle to the shores of Dunardee
5 I miss the river Shannon and the folks at Skibbereen
The moorlands and the meadows with their forty shades of green

But most of all I miss a girl in
10 Tipperary town
And most of all I miss her lips as soft as eiderdown
Again I want to see and do the things we've done and seen
15 Where the breeze is sweet as Shalimar and there's forty shades of green

I wish that I could spend an hour at Dublin's churning surf
20 I'd love to watch the farmers drain the bogs and spade the turf
To see again the thatching of the straw the women glean
I'd walk from Cork to Larne to see the
25 forty shades of green

But most of all I miss a girl in Tipperary town
And most of all I miss her lips as soft as eiderdown
Again, I want to see and do the things
30 we've done and seen
Where the breeze is sweet as Shalimar and there's forty shades of green

Annotations
12 **eiderdown** [ˈaɪdədaʊn] warm bedcover filled with feathers
16 **Shalimar** a French perfume
19 **churning surf** *(here)* waves rolling in
21 **bog** area of wet, muddy ground that is formed of dead plants
23 **glean sth.** collect sth.

Comprehension

1 a On a map of Ireland, mark the locations that are mentioned in the song.
  b Describe the image of Ireland created in the song.

Analysis

2 Analyse the *speaker's emotions and feelings.

Language awareness

3 a Ireland is referred to as 'the emerald of the sea' (l. 2). Explain this *metaphor and research the story of how Ireland came to be known as 'the Emerald Isle'.
  b Find a photo depicting an interesting aspect of Irish life and write a suitable caption describing Ireland metaphorically. Present your photos and captions in class.

▶ SF 13: Doing research, Student's book p. 278

Beyond the text

4 **You choose** Work on either task **a** or **b**.
  a Give reasons why 'Forty shades of green' may have been so popular for many decades. Does the song appeal to you, too?
  b There are many popular songs about Ireland. Find one that you particularly like. Why does it appeal to you?

▶ Getting started (task b)

  c **Speaking** Read the Info box on page 24. Then choose one of the protest songs mentioned in the text and investigate the story behind the song. What other perspectives on Ireland do these songs offer? Report back to class.

▶ SF 13: Doing research, Student's book p. 278

Text 8/9

Info

Irish protest songs – an intriguing part of Ireland's musical tradition

Ireland has a very rich musical tradition, and protest songs are an intrinsic part of it. Throughout history, music has helped the Irish express their national identity and give voice to those who would fight against injustice. Many modern Irish songs prove that this tradition lives on today. Protest songs dealing with
5 more recent aspects of Irish history include 'Banana Republic' (1980) by the Boomtown Rats, 'Sunday Bloody Sunday' (1983) by U2, 'Streets of Sorrow/ Birmingham Six' (1988) by The Pogues, 'This Is a Rebel Song' (1997) by Sinead O'Connor and 'Dublin Town' by Damien Dempsey (from 1997).

1 Choose one of the protest songs and find out what it's criticizing.

Text 9

Democratic disruption. Ireland's colonial hangover Bill Rolston

- On the first-ever state visit of a President of the Republic of Ireland to the United Kingdom in April 2014, President Michael D. Higgins (cf. info box on p. 25) described the relationship between the two nations as follows: 'Ireland and Britain live in both the shadow and in the shelter of one another, and so it has been since the dawn of history.' Explain this quote in your own words. Then share what you know about the 'shadows' and 'shelters' connecting the two countries. The pictures can help you.

Now read the text by Bill Rolston, a Northern Irish scholar. Much of his research deals with Ireland's ways of coping with its past.

In 1991 a Northern Ireland based NGO, the Centre for Research and Documentation, organised a conference in Dublin titled 'Is Ireland a Third World Country?' The question [...] was deliberately provocative. In one sense, the answer was clearly 'no'.
5 Ireland is not in the Global South. Dublin is the capital of a sovereign democratic state. There were economic problems, but no one was starving to death openly on the streets. And although a relatively low-intensity war [was] happening, it was happening in Northern Ireland, the part which stayed integrated in the
10 British political system when Ireland was partitioned in the 1920s.

On the other hand, in those years before the economic boom, known as 'the Celtic Tiger', the southern part of the island of Ireland was a very different place from what it is now. In 1841 the population of the whole, unpartitioned island was about
15 eight million. A devastating famine followed where two million or more died or emigrated. A century and a half later, despite a birth rate higher than [in] most other European countries, the population was less than six million. Even today,

Annotations
15 **famine** shortage of food

after the arrival of tens of thousands of European Union citizens and others, the island's population has not yet reached the pre-Famine level. The main reason for low population figures during the 90s was the extent of emigration. London, New York, Melbourne were teeming with young Irish people holding down successful jobs. They were not able to thrive in Ireland where employment opportunities were severely restricted. Economically, Ireland was acknowledged as the basket case of the European Union.

The colonisation of Ireland

When the South of Ireland achieved independence from Britain in 1922, it carried the baggage of centuries of colonial rule. The Normans had begun to conquer Ireland in the late 12th century. For the next five hundred years there was an uneasy relationship between Ireland and England which involved both incorporation and resistance. The Elizabethans determined to complete the conquest in the late 17th century, subduing the northern clans through a combination of war and plantation. Throughout much of the 18th and 19th centuries, English laws blocked the development of any indigenous industry which might challenge English economic dominance. Repressive control was 'normal' as resistance against conquest continued; in the second half of the 19th century the rule of law, unencumbered by emergency or martial measures, existed for only five years. Resistance reached its zenith with the Easter Rising in 1916, which was followed by the War of Independence from 1919 to 1921, the Treaty and the Government of Ireland Act 1920 which led to the partition of the island. The 26 southern counties – the Free State – were now a dominion within the British sphere of influence, while the six northern counties – Northern Ireland – had its own parliament but remained fully incorporated within the United Kingdom.

Repressive control and monopoly of power

The newly 'independent' Free State in the south was not really so. The young state would in time flex its muscles: it refused to join the British Commonwealth and declared military neutrality, it supported China, Palestine and Cuba in the United Nations; and in 1949 it declared itself a republic. But it was in many ways still a neo-colonial set-up.

The situation in Northern Ireland remained much more obviously colonial after 1921. In an attempt at counterinsurgency in the early 17th century, thousands of settlers had been brought in. Scottish, English-speaking and Presbyterian they had displaced the Gaelic-speaking, Catholic Irish from their land and the repercussions remain to this day. In 1921, the newly partitioned state got its own government, albeit subordinate to Britain, where the unionists, ultimately descendants from the original settlers, established a monopoly on power and control. Laws and policies kept the Catholics, ultimately the descendants of the original displaced indigenous, down. They experienced discrimination in the exercise of democratic rights, in access to employment and public housing, and a much higher rate of emigration. Eventually a civil rights campaign in the late 1960s morphed into a three-way war between pro-United Ireland nationalists, pro-British unionists, and British armed forces.

Annotations
31 **plantation** colonization
33 **indigenous** *(here)* local
35 **unencumbered** without any burden
50 **counterinsurgency** military actions against revolutionaries
51 **Presbyterian** member of the Presbyterian church, a Protestant Christian church
52 **Gaelic** Celtic language spoken in Ireland, Wales and Scotland
53 **repercussion** effect
54 **albeit** [ˌɔːlˈbiːɪt] although
54 **unionist** *(here)* supporter of Northern Ireland's union with Great Britain

Proclamation of Irish Independence during the Easter Rising 1916

Text 9

Annotations
70 **in perpetuity** forever
73 **intransigence** stubbornness; the quality in people not willing to compromise

Ireland's legacy of colonialism

But it is not simply about the past. The legacy of colonialism continues to work
65 itself out on the island of Ireland and especially in the north. A substantial proportion of the nationalist (Catholic) population regard the partition of the island a century ago as an imperial move that stranded them in a state in which they had no desire to belong. The state was built on inequality. When the unionists were planning where to draw the border, they opted for an area which would, in their words,
70 guarantee them 'a Protestant majority in perpetuity'. The roots of the low-intensity war from 1969 to 1994 are in that experience. The conflict was kick-started by demands for equality in a Civil Rights campaign in the late 1960s which was met with state intransigence and repression.

To this day, demands for equality continue to disrupt the operations of the state.
75 For example, a power-sharing government and executive which resulted from the peace agreement, the Good Friday Agreement, of 1998, collapsed in 2016 over a number of issues, including strong evidence of the corruption of unionist politicians. The other main partner in the executive, the republicans, withdrew over this and other issues. Another example is the determination of the unionists to block
80 an Irish Language Act. Gaelic has declined in many of the areas where it was once dominant, especially in the rural west of Ireland. But it has grown exponentially in urban areas in the north. There are language acts in the Irish Republic, Scotland and Wales protecting indigenous languages. The north is the only outlier, and that because of unionist intransigence. This is one of the reasons the republicans are in
85 no hurry to re-establish the power-sharing institutions.

For all that Ireland is not a developing country, it bears scars similar to those of other post-colonial countries in the Global South. It was colonised, and the legacy of colonialism continues to disrupt democratic processes to the present day. The process of decolonisation remains incomplete, most obviously in Northern Ireland
90 but also in the Republic. As Brexit threatens the economics and politics of these two neighbours, Britain and Ireland, there are many commentators who now argue that Ireland's economic development and political health depend on the ending of partition and the reunification of the country within the European Union. This would be a significant step on the road to decolonisation.

From: https://blogs.lse.ac.uk

Hands Across the Divide monument, symbolizing the reconciliation between Protestants and Catholics in the Northern Ireland conflict

▶ Getting started

▶ Check

▶ Support p. 29

▶ SF 17: Reading and understanding non-fictional texts, Student's book p. 285

Comprehension

1 a Read the text. Then put the following events from Irish history in chronological order:
Brexit • Good Friday Agreement • Irish Famine • Irish Free State • Partition • troubles in Northern Ireland • Celtic Tiger • Republic of Ireland.
b Read the text again and make notes on the events in **a**.
c 📖 Summarize the colonial legacies that, in the author's view, are still affecting Ireland today.

Analysis

2 Examine the author's intent in writing this article.

Language awareness

3 a Explain how the author's view of Irish history is reflected in his choice of the phrases 'the basket case of the European Union' (l. 23 f.) and 'the island of Ireland' (l. 13).
  b Find another sentence in the article reflecting the author's position through his choice of words. Rewrite it using more neutral words.

Beyond the text

4 Writing Write a comment on another quote by Irish President Michael D. Higgins, published in *The Guardian* in 2021. Bear the guiding question in mind.

▶ SF 26: Argumentative writing, Student's book p. 298

> It is vital to understand the nature of the British imperialist mindset of that time if we are to understand the history of coexisting support for, active resistance to, and, for most, a resigned acceptance of British rule in Ireland. While our nations have been utterly transformed over the past century, I suggest that there are important benefits for all on these islands of engaging with the shadows cast by our shared past.

Info

Michael D. Higgins (born 1941), a socialist, poet, academic and human rights advocate, was inaugurated as the 9th President of Ireland in 2011. On several occasions President Higgins has criticized British imperialism and the refusal of British academic institutions and media organizations to address its colonial
5 legacy. He believes that the distressing aspects of Britain's and Ireland's shared history need to be acknowledged to create a better future for both countries.

▶ More info

Chapter task

A time capsule is a box containing items that store essential information for future generations.
Create a time capsule for an English-speaking country using written information.

1. Form groups of four. Each group chooses one country you dealt with in this chapter. Choose five items that could help future generations understand this country's past and present and put them in a box.
2. Present your items in class and comment on them. What story does your time capsule tell?

Support and Partner B

Text 1

▶ p. 10

Does Britain need a museum of colonialism?

5 c Support

In your discussion, you may address the following aspects:
- what Britain's past mistakes were
- how it treated conquered peoples and nations
- what it should do to make up for past mistakes
- how similar mistakes could be avoided
- what today's major powers –the United States, China, the European Union– could learn from the British experience
- what international relations should be like today
- what nations could do to build lasting peace.

Text 2

▶ p. 11

Germany's colonial legacy

2 Support

Use the words in the box to generate ideas.

> **Language help**
>
> issue an apology • give development aid • build a monument • talk to victims' families • acknowledge/recognize sth. • compensate for sth. • pay reparations • educate sb. about sth.

Text 4

▶ p. 13

Welcome to Nigeria!

Partner B

- **Partner B:** What aspects of Nigerian life are depicted in the picture below and the one on the next page? Which picture comes closer to your notion of Nigeria?

Glimpses of the English-Speaking World

Support and Partner B

Go back to p. 13.

Text 5

My vision of Nigeria
▶ p. 16

2 Support

In your analysis, consider the following aspects:
- how often Ms. Yesufu refers to 'Nigeria' and 'Nigerians'
- how often she refers to Nigeria's separate ethnic groups
- which other proper names she uses in the text
- who she means by 'we'.

Text 9

Democratic disruption. Ireland's colonial hangover
▶ p. 26

2 Support

In your analysis, consider the following aspects:
- Statements of opinion or emotional appeals are often used by authors to persuade readers of their own opinions.
- Humorous details and personal anecdotes are often used to create interest, to entertain or to lend credibility to what is said.
- Descriptive passages or statistics are used to inform readers.

Which strategies are employed in the given text?

Abbreviations and labels used in *Context*

AE/BE	American English / British English	🗺️	marks tasks that refer you back to the chapter's guiding question
ca. *(Latin)*	circa = about, approximately		
cf.	confer (compare), see	**Challenge**	marks a more difficult task
derog	derogatory *(abfällig, geringschätzig)*		
e.g. *(Latin)*	exempli gratia = for example	▶ Support	refers you to the Support and Partner B pages (p. 28f.) where you can find more help to do the assignment
esp.	especially		
et al. *(Latin)*	et alii = and other people/things	**You choose**	lets you decide which of the two given assignments you'd like to do
etc. *(Latin)*	et cetera = and so on		
f./ff.	and the following page(s)/line(s)	**Intercultural communication**	marks a task that focuses on intercultural communication
fml	formal English		
i.e. *(Latin)*	id est = that is, in other words	*metaphor	indicates that a word or expression (here: *metaphor*) is explained in the Glossary in the Student's book *Context*, p. 334ff.
infml	informal English		
jdm./jdn.	*jemandem/jemanden*		
l./ll.	line/lines	▶ SF 48: Paraphrasing	directs you to the Skills File in the Student's book *Context*, p. 264ff. (here: Skill 48)
n	noun		
pt(s)	point(s)	🔊	indicates that the sound file can be found in the Cornelsen Lernen App, eBook and UMA
p./pp.	page/pages		
pl	plural	▶️	indicates that the video can be found in the Cornelsen Lernen App, eBook and UMA
sb./sth.	somebody/something		
sin	singular	▶ More info ⇩	indicates that additional information can be found in the Cornelsen Lernen App
sl	slang		
usu.	usually	▶ More language ⇩	indicates that tips or further information regarding language can be found in the Cornelsen Lernen App
v	verb		
vs.	*(Latin)* versus *(gegen, im Gegensatz zu)*	▶ Check ⇩	indicates that solutions to tasks can be found in the Cornelsen Lernen App
		▶ Getting started ⇩	indicates that tips or ideas to get started on tasks can be found in the Cornelsen Lernen App

Acknowledgements

Cover
Shutterstock.com/mehdi33300

Photos
pp. 4/5 and details: mauritius images/Art Collection 2/Alamy Stock Photos; **p. 9:** stock.adobe.com/Chris Sharp; **p. 10:** mauritius images/World Book Inc.; **p. 12**: Shutterstock.com/Luketaibai; **p. 13** top: stock.adobe.com/Bassey, bottom left map and flag: stock.adobe.com/Khaiinauy, people icons: Shutterstock.com/Design Collection, bottom right: stock.adobe.com/Fela Sanu; **p. 14** top: Shutterstock.com/saw graf, bottom: dpa Picture-Alliance/REUTERS/X02952/JOE PENNEY; **p. 16**: mauritius images/alamy stock photo/Majority World CIC; **p. 17** left: stock.adobe.com/Noppasinw, right: stock.adobe.com/Zerophoto; **p. 18**: ClipDealer GmbH/Andriy Kravchenko; **p. 19**: Shutterstock.com/haireena; **p. 21**: mauritius images/alamy stock photo/Kiyoshi Hijiki; **p. 22**: mauritius images/TopFoto; **p. 24** top: mauritius images/alamy stock photo/Magdalena Gierlik, bottom: Imago Stock & People GmbH/imageBROKER/Matthias Graben; **p. 25**: mauritius images/World Book Inc.; **p. 26**: mauritius images/alamy stock photo/Zoonar GmbH; **p. 27**: mauritius images/alamy stock photo/Graham Service; **p. 28**: stock.adobe.com/Terver, **p. 29**: stock.adobe.com/Артем Малахов

Texts
pp. 8–9 Flood, Alison. "UK needs a museum of colonialism, says historian William Dalrymple", *theguardian.com*, 16.09.2020, https://www.theguardian.com/books/2020/sep/16/uk-needs-a-museum-of-colonialism-says-historian-william-dalrymple (accessed 11.10.2021), Copyright Guardian News & Media Ltd 2021; **pp. 14–16**: Yesufu, Aisha. "The Nigeria That I See". *Remaking Nigeria. Sixty Years, Sixty Voices.*, edited by Chido Onumah, Premium Times Books, 2020, pp. 44–49; **p. 19**: Lo Wei Wei, Miriam. "Bumboat Cruise on the Singapore River." Westerly 50, Westerly Magazine, 2005, pp. 87–88; **pp. 20–22**: "Digitaler Stadtstaat: Wie Singapur zur Smart Nation wurde", *FAZ*, 31.05.2021, Christoph Hein © Alle Rechte vorbehalten. Frankfurter Allgemeine Zeitung GmbH, Frankfurt. Zur Verfügung gestellt vom Frankfurter Allgemeine Archiv; **pp. 24–26**: Rolston, Bill. "Democratic disruption. Ireland's colonial hangover." LSE, 5 Jul. 2019, blogs.lse.ac.uk/wps/2019/07/05/democratic-disruption-irelands-colonial-hangover (accessed 8.10. 2021); **p. 24** Quote by Michael D. Higgins: Higgins, Michael D. "Irish President Michael D Higgins's toast at the Queen's state banquet: In full." *Belfast Telegraph*, 8 Apr. 2014. Accessed 16 December 2021; **p. 27**: Quote by Higgins, Michael D. "Empire shaped Ireland's past. A century after partition, it still shapes our present." *theguardian.com*, 11 Feb. 2021, www.theguardian.com/commentisfree/2021/feb/11/empire-ireland-century-partition-present-britain-history (accessed 8.10.2021)

Song
p. 23: *Forty Shades of Green*. Copyright Warner Chappell Music GmbH & Co. KG Germany/Text, (OT) Cash, Johnny

Topics in Context

Context

Saving the Planet – Our Future at Risk

Themenheft

Cornelsen

Context

Saving the Planet – Our Future at Risk

Im Auftrag des Verlages herausgegeben von
Dr. Annette Leithner-Brauns, Dresden

Erarbeitet von
Martina Baasner, Berlin; Irene Bartscherer, Bonn; Lisa Braun, Meppen; Dr. Sabine Buchholz, Hürth; Wiebke Bettina Dietrich, Göttingen; Sylvia Loh, Esslingen; Benjamin Lorenz, Bensheim; Dr. Paul Maloney, Hildesheim; Dr. Pascal Ohlmann, Tholey; Birgit Ohmsieder, Berlin; Dr. Andreas Sedlatschek, Esslingen; Veronika Walther, Rudolstadt

In Zusammenarbeit mit der Englischredaktion
Dr. Marion Kiffe (Koordinierende Redakteurin), Dr. Christiane Kallenbach (Projektleitung), Aryane Beaudoin, Dr. Jan Dreßler, Hartmut Tschepe, Dr. Christian von Raumer, Freya Wurm *unter Mitwirkung von* Janan Barksdale, Irja Fröhling, Katrin Gütermann, Anne Müller, Neil Porter, Evelyn Sternad, Mai Weber

Beratende Mitwirkung
Ramin Azadian, Berlin; Heiko Benzin, Neustrelitz; Sabine Otto, Halle (Saale)

Layoutkonzept
Klein & Halm, Berlin

Layout und technische Umsetzung
Straive
designcollective, Berlin

Umschlaggestaltung
Rosendahl, Berlin

Lizenzmanagement
Britta Bensmann

Weitere Bestandteile des Lehrwerks

- *Schulbuch* (print und als E-Book)
- *E-Books* (in zwei Varianten: 1. alle *Topics in Context* bzw. 2. Schulbuch und *Topics in Context*)
- *Lehrkräftefassung des Schulbuchs* (im Unterrichtsmanager)
- *Handreichungen für den Unterricht* (print und im Unterrichtsmanager)
- *Workbook* (print)
- *Unterrichtsmanager*
- *Vorschläge zur Leistungsmessung* (digital)
- *Cornelsen Lernen App*

---

www.cornelsen.de

Die Webseiten Dritter, deren Internetadressen in diesem Lehrwerk angegeben sind, wurden vor Drucklegung sorgfältig geprüft. Der Verlag übernimmt keine Gewähr für die Aktualität und den Inhalt dieser Seiten oder solcher, die mit ihnen verlinkt sind.

1. Auflage, 1. Druck 2022

Alle Drucke dieser Auflage sind inhaltlich unverändert und können im Unterricht nebeneinander verwendet werden.

© 2022 Cornelsen Verlag GmbH, Berlin

Das Werk und seine Teile sind urheberrechtlich geschützt. Jede Nutzung in anderen als den gesetzlich zugelassenen Fällen bedarf der vorherigen schriftlichen Einwilligung des Verlages. Hinweis zu §§ 60 a, 60 b UrhG: Weder das Werk noch seine Teile dürfen ohne eine solche Einwilligung an Schulen oder in Unterrichts- und Lehrmedien (§ 60 b Abs. 3 UrhG) vervielfältigt, insbesondere kopiert oder eingescannt, verbreitet oder in ein Netzwerk eingestellt oder sonst öffentlich zugänglich gemacht oder wiedergegeben werden. Dies gilt auch für Intranets von Schulen.

Druck: H. Heenemann, Berlin

ISBN 978-3-06-035865-6

PEFC zertifiziert
Dieses Produkt stammt aus nachhaltig bewirtschafteten Wäldern und kontrollierten Quellen.
www.pefc.de
PEFC/04-31-1156

Contents

Title	Topic	Text type / media	Skills	Page
Lead-in				6
Words in Context: Our planet is in danger	Planet Earth under threat	Informative text		8
Text 1: Climate activism *Greta Thunberg* *Prince Ea*	Environmental awareness Fighting climate change	Speech Poem (Partner B)	Speaking	10
Text 2: Scientists warn of a global climate emergency *Phoebe Weston*	Climate change	Newspaper article	Writing	11
Info box: The Paris Agreement	Ecological policies	Informative text		14
Text 3: After the storm *Jesmyn Ward* **Art in Context:** Drowned City	Devastation through Hurricane Katrina	Novel extract Extract from a graphic novel	Creative writing	15
Text 4: The future of energy *Steven Chu*	Resources and the future of energy	Video	Listening Viewing Writing	19
Text 5: Green city Singapore *Amy Kolczak*	Urban development in Singapore	Newspaper article	Writing	20
Text 6: What shall we eat? *Jonathan Safran Foer*	Clashes of interest	Extract from non-fiction book	Speaking Writing	22
Text 7: Sustainability at German schools *Anima Müller*	Sustainability	Newspaper article	Mediating	25
Chapter Task: An ecoproject			Speaking	27
Support and Partner B				28
Acknowledgements				32

Contents

Abbreviations and labels used in *Context*

AE/BE	American English / British English
ca. *(Latin)*	circa = about, approximately
cf.	confer (compare), see
derog	derogatory *(abfällig, geringschätzig)*
e.g. *(Latin)*	exempli gratia = for example
esp.	especially
et al. *(Latin)*	et alii = and other people/things
etc. *(Latin)*	et cetera = and so on
f./ff.	and the following page(s)/line(s)
fml	formal English
i.e. *(Latin)*	id est = that is, in other words
infml	informal English
jdm./jdn.	*jemandem/jemanden*
l./ll.	line/lines
n	noun
pt(s)	point(s)
p./pp.	page/pages
pl	plural
sb./sth.	somebody/something
sin	singular
sl	slang
usu.	usually
v	verb
vs.	*(Latin)* versus *(gegen, im Gegensatz zu)*

🗺	marks tasks that refer you back to the chapter's guiding question
Challenge	marks a more difficult task
▶ **Support**	refers you to the Support and Partner B pages (p. 28ff.) where you can find more help to do the assignment
You choose	lets yo decide which of the two given assignments you'd like to do
Intercultural communication	marks a task that focuses on intercultural communication
* metaphor	indicates that a word or expression (here: *metaphor*) is explained in the Glossary in the Student's book *Context*, p. 334ff.
▶ SF 48: Paraphrasing	directs you to the Skills File in the Student's book *Context*, p. 264ff. (here: Skill 48)
🔊	indicates that the sound file can be found in the Cornelsen Lernen App, eBook and UMA
▶️	indicates that the video can be found in the Cornelsen Lernen App, eBook and UMA
▶ More info	indicates that additional information can be found in the Cornelsen Lernen App
▶ More language	indicates that tips or further information regarding language can be found in the Cornelsen Lernen App
▶ Check	indicates that solutions to tasks can be found in the Cornelsen Lernen App
▶ Getting started	indicates that tips or ideas to get started on tasks can be found in the Cornelsen Lernen App

Saving the Planet – Our Future at Risk

▶ Getting started

▶ SF 22: Analysing visuals, Student's book p. 292

1 Choose either the left or the right half of the picture above.
   a **Think** Make notes for a description of your half of the picture.

   > **Language help**
   >
   > make sb. think of … • refer/allude to … • suggest/symbolize sth. … • connect sth. to the idea of … • be in / out of balance • flourishing • natural habitat • wildlife • in balance • harmonious living • catastrophic event • ecological disaster • wildfire • hurricane • drought • out of control • devastating • lush

   b **Pair** Find a partner who has chosen the other half of the picture. Describe your pictures to each other and discuss their messages.
   c **Share** Discuss in class: What kind of future are we and our planet heading for?

2 Look at the Chapter map on the right: How might the guiding question in the middle and the elements around it be related? What can they tell you about this chapter?

Chapter map

environmentalism

extreme weather events

climate change

Chapter task: an ecoproject ✓

There is no Planet B – how can we save Planet A?

renewable energy

greener cities

sustainable lifestyles

Words in Context

▶ More language

🔊 ## Our planet is in danger

At the crossroads
The ecology of planet Earth has never been in complete balance. Rather, there have always been times when certain groups of animals or plants multiplied to such an extent that they used up too many resources. In the end, not all of them were able to
5 survive, which in turn gave their resources the opportunity to recover and the circle could start anew. These small disturbances in the earth's ecological balance never actually threatened its equilibrium. But as we humans have increased in number, and as scientific and technological progress has enabled us to modify our planet according to our ever-growing needs, we are on the way to destroying the basis of our livelihood to
10 such an extent that the survival of the human species and other species with it is in jeopardy. So it's up to us humans to make a significant change.

Climate change – vital signs of the planet
Throughout history, the earth's climate has undergone changes. But since the Industrial Revolution, when people began burning fossil fuels on a massive scale, our
15 atmosphere has changed, causing the globe to heat up at an unprecedented rate. Scientific evidence shows that humankind is responsible for the biggest climate change in history. Some of the effects that pose the greatest threat are the rise in global temperatures, increasing levels of carbon dioxide, warming of the oceans, the ongoing loss of sea ice, and rising sea levels worldwide. Extreme weather events, such
20 as hurricanes, wildfires, severe droughts or floods, are also becoming increasingly frequent.

Sustainability – resources and the future of energy
Scientists predict that a rise in global temperatures of more than 2°C compared to pre-industrial levels will have catastrophic consequences for billions of people around
25 the world. Gradually, people are becoming aware of the environmental crisis. In 2015, governments signed the Paris Agreement in which they agreed to limit global warming to 2°C, and, if possible, to keep it below 1.5°C. To achieve this goal, we first of all need to drastically reduce CO_2 emissions. This can only be achieved by finding and developing cheap zero-carbon ways to generate electricity, produce things and grow
30 food. Variable energy sources like solar, wind and water power can play a substantial role. Many of today's ecological problems are caused by the industrialized countries; they will need to take the lead in solving these problems. As the global population is likely to reach 10 billion by 2100, we are going to need more energy and food for everyone.

35 ### Our options – a vision for the future
There are voices claiming that we're close to certain tipping points, i.e. thresholds beyond which complete ecosystems will be harmed beyond repair, causing unpredictable changes to the world's climate. Many people believe that there is still a chance of saving the planet and thereby the wellbeing of future generations. But they all agree
40 that this requires a huge effort and will not be easy. Action also needs to be taken immediately. Politicians and governments will have to work together, raise the price of emitting CO_2, and invest in renewable energy sources etc. However, it is also up to each one of us to find more sustainable ways of living, protect our unique wildlife, restore endangered ecosystems, use clean energy and recycle our waste.

Words in Context

1 **Words words words**

   a   Find three highlighted words or phrases in the text that are important to the topic of saving the planet and/or were new to you.

   b   Explain these words or phrases in English. Use a dictionary if necessary.

   c   Work with a partner: One person presents an explanation, the other guesses the word/phrase. Add at least one word/phrase along with its explanation to your original three.

▶ Getting started

2 **A spidergram**

Collect useful words from the text and arrange them in a spidergram. You may also include the words from **a**.

3 **Chunk it!**

Words are commonly grouped together with two or more words so as to form *chunks.

   a   Find adjectives or verbs that are often used with the following words to form chunks. You can check the text for help, but also add other words. If you are not sure, use a dictionary.
   1   environment
   2   fossil fuels
   3   CO_2 emissions
   4   global warming
   5   ecosystem
   6   energy

   b   Check your chunks with a partner and add new ones to your list.

4 **Talking to a radio reporter**

Look at the second paragraph, 'Climate change – vital signs of the planet'. Use that paragraph as the basis for a short statement you might give to a radio reporter at a *Fridays for Future* gathering.

   a   Work with a partner and collect ideas.
   b   Write down your statement.

Language help

absolutely important • be totally convinced that ... • There is no doubt that ... • There is no denying the fact that ...

There is no Planet B – how can we save Planet A?

Text 1

Climate activism   Greta Thunberg

- Do you personally know anybody who is environmentally aware and tries to get others involved? Tell your class about them and about what they do.

You are going to read texts by Greta Thunberg and Prince Ea — two people who are speaking out against climate change.

Partner B: Turn to p. 28. **Partner A:** Read the text below. Work on tasks **1–3**.

On 23 September 2019, environmental activist Greta Thunberg addressed the UN.

This is all wrong. I shouldn't be standing here.

I should be back in school on the other side of the ocean. Yet you all come to us young people for hope? How dare you!

You have taken away my dreams and my childhood with your empty words. And yet I'm one of the lucky ones.

People are suffering. People are dying. Entire ecosystems are collapsing. We are in the beginning of a mass extinction. And all you can talk about is money and fairy tales of eternal economic growth. How dare you!

For more than 30 years the science has been crystal clear. How dare you continue to look away, and come here saying that you're doing enough.

When the politics and solutions needed are still nowhere in sight.

You say you 'hear' us and that you understand the urgency. But no matter how sad and angry I am, I do not want to believe that. Because if you fully understood the situation and still kept on failing to act, then you would be evil. And I refuse to believe that.

The popular idea of cutting our emissions in half in ten years only gives us a 50 per cent chance of staying below 1.5°C and the risk of setting off irreversible chain reactions beyond human control.

Fifty per cent may be acceptable to you.

But since those numbers do not include tipping points, most feedback loops, additional warming hidden by toxic air pollution, nor the aspect of equity, then a 50 per cent risk is simply not acceptable to us, we who have to live with the consequences. We do not accept these odds.

To have a 67 per cent chance of staying below a 1.5°C global temperature rise, the best odds given by the IPCC, the world had 420 gigatonnes of CO_2 left to emit back on 1 January 2018.

Today that figure is already down to less than 350 gigatonnes. How dare you pretend that this can be solved with just business as usual and some technical solutions!

With today's emissions levels, that remaining CO_2 budget will be entirely gone within less than 8.5 years.

There will not be any solutions or plans presented in line with these figures here today. Because these numbers are too uncomfortable. And you are still not mature enough to tell it like it is.

▶ More info

Annotations

- 3 **How dare you!** *Was fällt Ihnen ein! / Wie können Sie es wagen!*
- 7 **mass extinction** situation in which 75% of species are lost
- 7 **fairytale** story sb. tells that is not true; lie
- 12 **urgency** necessity to deal with a situation immediately
- 17 **set sth. off** cause sth. to begin
- 20 **tipping point** time at which a change or effect suddenly reach a point at which they cannot be stopped
- 20 **feedback loop** self-reinforcing factors in a process
- 21 **equity** justice, fairness
- 32 **mature** *(adj)* grown-up

Text 1/2

You are failing us. But the young people are starting to understand your betrayal.
35 The eyes of all future generations are upon you.

And if you choose to fail us I say: We will never forgive you.

We will not let you get away with this. Right here, right now is where we draw the line.

The world is waking up. And change is coming, whether you like it or not.

From: No One Is too Small to Make a Difference, *2019*

Annotations
34 **fail sb.** let sb. down, disappoint sb.
34 **betrayal** treachery

Comprehension

1 For your partner, summarize the main message of the text.

▶ Check

Analysis

2 **a** Analyse the *stylistic devices used in your text.
   b Choose two examples and present them to your partner.

▶ Support p. 31

Beyond the text

3 **a** Explain to your partner why you think your text is convincing and likely to inspire others to take action or not.
   b Discuss which of the texts you would use as an introduction to an eco-project.

4 Do some research on other people trying to save the planet. Your ideas for the guiding question may give you some inspiration. Name the activist who you think is the most impressive and convincing. Give reasons for your answer.

▶ Getting started

Text 2

Scientists warn of a global climate emergency
Phoebe Weston

- Explain the word *emergency*. What do you associate with it?

Now read the following text about different aspects of a global climate emergency.

The planet is facing a 'ghastly future of mass extinction, declining health and climate-disruption upheavals' that threaten human survival because of ignorance and inaction, according to an international group of scientists, who warn people still haven't grasped the urgency of the biodiversity and climate crises.

5 The 17 experts, including Prof Paul Ehrlich from Stanford University, author of *The Population Bomb*, and scientists from Mexico, Australia and the US, say the planet is in a much worse state than most people – even scientists – understood.

'The scale of the threats to the biosphere and all its lifeforms – including humanity – is in fact so great that it is difficult to grasp for even well-informed experts,'
10 they write in a report in *Frontiers in Conservation Science* which references more than 150 studies detailing the world's major environmental challenges.

The delay between destruction of the natural world and the impacts of these actions means people do not recognise how vast the problem is, the paper argues.

Annotations
1 **ghastly** very frightening and threatening
2 **climate disruption** profound change to the climate that threatens the continuation of life on earth in the normal way
2 **upheaval** radical change
4 **grasp sth.** understand sth.
4 **urgency** need to be dealt with quickly
8 **scale** size
12 **delay** period of time between one thing and another
13 **vast** extremely big

Text 2

Annotations

- 14 **magnitude** extreme size
- 15 **fabric** structure that allows sth. to function properly
- 18 **surrender** give up
- 23 **perpetual** never-ending
- 23 **externalities** effects of production and consumption
- 24 **rein in sth.** keep sth. under control
- 26 **Aichi biodiversity target** targets for the protection of biodiversity agreed upon in 2010 at a conference in Aichi, Japan
- 27 **stem sth.** stop sth.
- 27 **the second consecutive time** the second time in a row
- 29 **pledge sth.** formally promise sth.
- 33 **imminent** likely to happen very soon
- 39 **equity** situation in which all people are treated in a fair manner
- 40 **junk** (infml) worthless stuff
- 41 **soil degradation** lessening of the quality of the uppermost layer of the earth, on which plants grow
- 45 **scarce** rare
- 48 **gravity** seriousness
- 55 **stark** marked

'[The] mainstream is having difficulty grasping the magnitude of this loss, despite
15 the steady erosion of the fabric of human civilisation.'

The report warns that climate-induced mass migrations, more pandemics and conflicts over resources will be inevitable unless urgent action is taken.

'Ours is not a call to surrender – we aim to provide leaders with a realistic "cold shower" of the state of the planet that is essential for planning to avoid a ghastly
20 future,' it adds.

Dealing with the enormity of the problem requires far-reaching changes to global capitalism, education and equality, the paper says. These include abolishing the idea of perpetual economic growth, properly pricing environmental externalities, stopping the use of fossil fuels, reining in corporate lobbying, and empowering
25 women, the researchers argue.

The report comes months after the world failed to meet a single UN Aichi biodiversity target, created to stem the destruction of the natural world, the second consecutive time governments have failed to meet their 10-year biodiversity goals. This week a coalition of more than 50 countries pledged to protect almost a third of the
30 planet by 2030.

An estimated one million species are at risk of extinction, many within decades, according to a recent UN report. [...]

In *The Population Bomb*, published in 1968, Ehrlich warned of imminent population explosion and hundreds of millions of people starving to death. Although he
35 has acknowledged some timings were wrong, he has said he stands by its fundamental message that population growth and high levels of consumption by wealthy nations is driving destruction.

He told the Guardian: 'Growthmania is the fatal disease of civilisation – it must be replaced by campaigns that make equity and well-being society's goals – not con-
40 suming more junk.'

Large populations and their continued growth drive soil degradation and biodiversity loss, the new paper warns. 'More people means that more synthetic compounds and dangerous throwaway plastics are manufactured, many of which add to the growing toxification of the Earth. It also increases the chances of pandemics
45 that fuel ever-more desperate hunts for scarce resources.'

The effects of the climate emergency are more evident than biodiversity loss, but still, society is failing to cut emissions, the paper argues. If people understood the magnitude of the crises, changes in politics and policies could match the gravity of the threat.

50 'Our main point is that once you realise the scale and imminence of the problem, it becomes clear that we need much more than individual actions like using less plastic, eating less meat, or flying less. Our point is that we need big systematic changes and fast,' Professor Daniel Blumstein from the University of California Los Angeles, who helped write the paper, told the Guardian. [...]

55 The report follows years of stark warnings about the state of the planet from the world's leading scientists, including a statement by 11,000 scientists in 2019 that

people will face 'untold suffering due to the climate crisis' unless major changes are made. [...] Prof Tom Oliver, an ecologist at the University of Reading, who was not involved in the report, said it was a frightening but credible summary of the grave threats society faces under a 'business as usual' scenario. 'Scientists now need to go beyond simply documenting environmental decline, and instead find the most effective ways to catalyse action,' he said.

Prof Rob Brooker, head of ecological sciences at the James Hutton Institute, who was not involved in the study, said it clearly emphasised the pressing nature of the challenges.

'We certainly should not be in any doubt about the huge scale of the challenges we are facing and the changes we will need to make to deal with them,' he said.

From: 'Top scientists warn of "ghastly future of mass extinction" and climate disruption', theguardian.com, 13 January 2021

Comprehension

1. Get together in groups of three.
   a. Each of you make notes on what the text says about one of the following:
      – factors that led to the climate emergency in the first place
      – the state of the world that justifies the label of a climate emergency
      – measures that should be taken to counteract the climate emergency.
   b. Tell the other group members what you found out.

▶ Getting started

Analysis

2. Work on either **a** or **b**.
   a. Analyse the structure of the text. It may help if you add a headline to each part you've identified.
   b. **Challenge** The text does not follow the conventional structure of an argumentative text. Analyse how it manages to express an opinion.

Language awareness

3. Work on either **a** or **b**.
   a. The scientists quoted in the article use a number of qualifying adjectives and adverbs that stress their idea of an emergency. Identify them.
   b. **Challenge** The choice of words used by the scientists quoted in the article stresses their idea of an emergency. Identify these words.
   c. Choose three examples from task **a** or **b** and rewrite them in a more matter-of-fact tone.

▶ More language (task a)

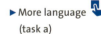

Beyond the text

4. Think back to your definitions of and associations with *emergency*. Discuss whether this term is justified with respect to the world's climate.

Text 2

5 📖 **Writing** Referring to Blumstein's view that individual actions are not enough to fight climate change (cf. ll. 50f.), a friend of yours announces on his blog that he finds it worthless to be environmentally responsible. Think back on your ideas from the guiding question, then write a passionate reply to your friend's post, arguing either for or against what he wrote. Make use of the strategies from task **3**.

▶ More info

Info

On 12 December 2015, 196 countries signed a legally binding international treaty on climate change, which is referred to as the **Paris Agreement**. The aim is for signatory countries to cooperate in environmental matters and, most importantly, to limit global warming to well below 2°C compared to preindustrial levels. The
5 treaty is a sign that political leaders have realized the importance of working together when our planet is faced with severe and irreversible damage.

Participating countries aim to reach a peak in global greenhouse gas emissions as soon as possible in order to achieve a climate neutral world by 2050. According to experts, this is the only way to stop global warming in time to prevent a planetary
10 catastrophe. The Paris Agreement is therefore considered a landmark in the fight against climate change. For the first time, a binding agreement attempts to engage all nations in a common effort to combat climate change and find innovative solutions for adapting to the effects of global warming.

However, this requires massive economic and social transformation based on the
15 best available science in order to implement the aims of the Paris Agreement and embed them in the political agendas of the different countries. In 2020, countries submitted their plans for climate action known as nationally determined contributions (NDCs). The EU submitted a common NDC. In these NDCs, each country commits to actions it will undertake to reduce its greenhouse gas emissions, as well
20 as actions to adapt and increase resilience to the impact of rising temperatures.

Hopefully an international treaty such as this will put more pressure on each individual nation to keep its promises when it comes to fighting climate change. One of its positive effects is that the treaty has raised environmental awareness and generated a huge amount of publicity about environmentalism, a topic that
25 is still too often ignored. People have come to realize that climate change action needs to be massively increased to achieve the goals of the Paris Agreement.

The agreement's entry into force has already sparked low-carbon solutions and new markets. More and more countries, regions, cities and companies are establishing carbon neutrality targets, and zero-carbon solutions are becoming com-
30 petitive across economic sectors. It is estimated that, by 2030, zero-carbon solutions could be competitive in sectors that are the source of over 70% of global emissions.

But there have also been drawbacks in the history of the treaty, as, for instance, in 2020 when the USA under President Donald Trump decided to withdraw from it.
35 In 2021, when President Biden took office, the USA rejoined.

1 What aims have different countries set themselves under the Paris Agreement?

14 Saving the Planet – Our Future at Risk

After the storm Jesmyn Ward

▶ More info
▶ Getting started

- Climate change is thought to make extreme weather events increasingly likely to happen. With a partner, talk about such weather events that you may have experienced or heard about. Describe what happened and how it made you feel.

> **Language help**
> drought • wildfire • lose your belongings • feel lost/afraid/hopeless • enormous/overwhelming/devastating damage • under water • flooded • destroyed • charred • burnt to the ground • uninhabitable • look for shelter • call for help • save yourself

Jesmyn Ward's novel Salvage the Bones (2011) follows an African American working-class family in southern Mississippi during the time of Hurricane Katrina (▶ Info box). The family consists of 15-year-old Esch (the narrator), her brothers Randall, Skeetah and Junior, and her father. When Katrina hits, they narrowly manage to escape from the floods surrounding their house. Later, when they return to what the storm has left of their home, the sight is disheartening.

[…] When the water left, the front part of Daddy's truck was sitting on top of the smashed gas tank. The lower half was on the ground. All the water that had been in the car was out, and it left a muddy slime on the windows. The yard was one big puddle that we waded, so icy at our ankles, the first cold water we'd felt since the
5 March rains, to the back door of the house, which was blasted open. The screen door was gone. The inside of the house was wet and muddy as Daddy's truck. The food we'd gotten had been washed from the shelves, and we hunted for it like we did for eggs, finding some silver cans of peas. We found Top Ramen, still sealed, in the sofa. We put them in our shirts. My hands were pink with Skeetah's blood from
10 hugging him earlier. I washed them in a puddle in the living room.

'We can't stay here. We need shelter.' Randall grimaced.

'Your hand, and the water …' Randall trailed off. 'Who knows what the water had in it.'

Daddy shook his head, his lips weak as a baby's. He looked dazed. He stared at his
15 truck, the ruined house, the yard invisible under the trees and the storm's deposits.

'Where,' he said, and it was a statement with no answer.

'By Big Henry,' Randall said.

Junior was on Randall's back, his eyes finally uncovered and open. He looked drunk.

20 'What about Skeet?' I asked.

'He'll find us,' Randall said. 'Daddy?' He raised an arm to Daddy, flicked his head towards the road.

'Yeah.' Daddy cleared his throat.

'We can fix it,' Randall said.

> **Info**
> When **Hurricane Katrina** hit the southeastern United States in late August, 2005, it claimed more than 1,800 lives, making it one of the severest natural disasters in U.S. history. On 29 August, the storm made landfall as a Category 4 hurricane in Louisiana near New Orleans. It then continued along the Mississippi Sound, where it slammed into coastal cities with a surge more than 8 metres high and destroyed thousands of homes. Many people without cars or not enough money to pay for public transport remained in the area at risk. Levees and flood walls having failed, people tried to escape from their flooded houses and find help. Some people could only be rescued several days after the storm had hit.

Annotations
8 **Top Ramen** brand of ready to cook noodles
14 **dazed** confused or unable to think clearly, esp. as a result of an injury or from shock

Text 3

Annotations

27 **gash** *(n)* cut, wound
34 **magnolia** type of tree or shrub with beautiful flowers
35 **ditch** *(n)* long narrow channel cut into the ground at the side of a road or field
37 **shingle** small flat piece of wood used to cover the roof or wall of a building
55 **machete** [məˈʃeti] broad heavy knife
61 **China** name of Skeetah's dog

25 Daddy looked down at the ground, shrugged. He glanced at me and shame filtered across his face like a spider, sideways, fast, and then he looked past the house to the road and started walking slowly, uneven, limping. There was a gash in the back of his leg, bleeding through his pants.

We picked our way round the fallen, ripped trees, to the road. We were barefoot, 30 and the asphalt was warm. We hadn't had time to find our shoes before the hand of the flood pushed into the living room. The storm had plucked the trees like grass and scattered them. We knew where the road was by the feel of the stones wearing through the blacktop under our feet; the trees I had known, the oaks in the bend, the stand of pines on the long stretch, the magnolia at the four-way, were all bro-35 ken, all crumbled. The sound of the water running in the ditches like rapids escorted us down the road, into the heart of Bois Sauvage.

The first house we saw was Javon's, the shingles of his roof scraped off, the top bald; the house was dark and looked empty until we saw someone who must have been Javon, light as Manny, standing in front of the pile of wood that must have 40 been the carport, lighting a lighter: a flicker of warmth in the cold air left by the storm. At the next nearest house, when the neighborhood started to cluster more closely together, we saw what others had suffered: every house had faced the hurricane, and every house had lost. Franco and his mother and father stood out in the yard looking at each other and the smashed landscape around them, dazed. Half of 45 their roof was gone. Christophe and Joshua's porch was missing, and part of their roof. A tree had smashed into Mudda Ma'am and Tilda's house. And just as the houses clustered, there were people in the street, barefoot, half naked, walking around felled trees, crumpled trampolines, talking with each other, shaking their heads, repeating one word over and over again: *alive, alive, alive, alive.* Big Henry 50 and Marquise were standing in front of Big Henry's house, which was missing a piece of its roof, like all the others, and was encircled by six of the trees that had stood in the yard but that now fenced the house in like a green gate.

'It's a miracle,' Big Henry said. 'All the trees fell away from the house.'

'We was just about to walk up there and see about y'all,' Marquise said.

55 Big Henry nodded, swung the machete he had in his hand, the blade dark and sharp.

'In case we had to cut through to get to y'all,' Marquise explained.

'Where's Skeet?' Big Henry asked.

'Looking,' Randall said, hoisting Junior farther up on his back.

60 'For what?' Marquise asked.

'The water took China,' I said.

'Water?' Big Henry asked, his voice high at the end, almost cracking.

'From the creek that feeds the pit,' Randall said. 'The house flooded through. We had to swim to the old house, wait out the storm in the attic.'

65 I wanted to say: We almost drowned. We had to bust out of the attic. We lost the puppies and China.

'We need a place to stay,' I said.

'It's just me and my mama,' Big Henry said. 'Plenty of room. Come on.' He flicked the machete blade, threw it to Marquise, who caught the handle and almost 70 dropped it.

'You all right, Mr Claude?' Big Henry asked Daddy.

Every line of Daddy's face, his shoulders, his neck, his collarbone, the ends of his arms, seemed to be caught in a net dragging the ground.

'Yeah,' Daddy said. 'I just need to sit for a while. My hand.'

75 He stopped short. Big Henry nodded, placed one of those big careful hands on Daddy's back, and escorted us through the milling crowd, the crumbled trees, the power lines tangled like abandoned fishing line, to his home. He looked at me over his shoulder, and the glance was so soft, so tentative and tender, I wanted to finish my story. I wanted to say, *I'm pregnant*. But I didn't. [...]

From: Salvage the Bones, *London, 2011*

Annotations
72 **collarbone**
Schlüsselbein
76 **mill around**
(v) (esp. of a group of people) walk around aimlessly
78 **tentative** timid, hesitant

Comprehension

1 Outline what happened to the *narrator and her family after the hurricane.

2 Describe the effect Hurricane Katrina had on Esch's home and neighbourhood.

Analysis

3 Analyse the way the author conveys the *protagonists' feelings and the emotional impact this has on the reader.

▶ Support p. 31

Language awareness

4 a Find examples of *informal style in the text and explain why the author uses it in her novel.
   b Rewrite at least two sentences in a more *formal style and compare the effect this has.

Beyond the text

5 Writing The neighbour asks Esch's father if he's alright (l. 71). Imagine he gave a genuine reply – what would he say? Write down his answer.

▶ SF 36: Creative writing, Student's book p. 311

Text 3

From: Don Brown, Drowned City, *2015*

▶ SF 22: Analysing visuals, Student's book p. 292

▶ More language

7 Art in Context Look at the picture from Don Brown's graphic novel about Hurricane Katrina.
   a Describe the picture and your first reactions to it.
   b The picture presents different aspects of the storm:
      • the wind's strength (cf. bending trees and flying roofs)
      • the damage done (cf. floating cars, houses under water)
      • a person's fear that they are not going to make it
      • the general atmosphere caused by the storm (cf. the greyish colours)
      • the storm's magnitude (cf. the bird's eye perspective)
      Try to identify passages in the novel excerpt you have read that also cover these aspects. Say whether they are better represented by the picture or the novel excerpt. Explain your choice.
   c What medium of storytelling (fiction, graphic novel, film, …) do you generally prefer and why? Discuss your ideas with a partner.

Text 4

The future of energy Steven Chu

Climate change is attributed to the excessive use of fossil fuels to provide humankind with energy. Sustainable, renewable sources of energy that do not threaten the climate are in use, but they all have their flipsides.

- Name sustainable sources of energy and say why their use may be limited.
- *Quick write:** Which sources of energy will be dominant by the end of the 21st century? Consider e.g. means of transportation, household appliances, heating, or the production of goods.

You are now going to hear Steven Chu, a Stanford professor of physics and cellular physiology, talk about the problems we are facing today and the solutions science and technology have to offer.

▶ Getting started

Info
Today, around 80% of the energy used worldwide to light and heat our homes, to produce gadgets in factories, or to fly around the world stems from **fossil fuels**. This energy is held responsible for around 80% of the greenhouse gas emissions that cause climate change.

Comprehension

1 Listening Listen to Steven Chu, then make notes on the following topics. Don't write complete sentences.
   1 one goal to be achieved by 2100 to fight climate change: …
   2 two ways to provide energy on demand: …
   3 two ways that batteries will have to be improved: …
   4 the source of energy used for transportation by 2100: …
   5 one promising policy to get away from fossil fuels: …
   6 three things that major oil companies have realized: …
   7 two consequences of rising sea levels: …

▶ Getting started

▶ SF 38: Listening/Viewing for gist and detail, Student's book p. 314.

Analysis

2 Listening Watch Chu's statement a second time. Examine how he proposes to instantly provide sufficient energy whenever it is demanded.

> **Language help**
> use a clear structure • be based on … • provide facts and figures • use expert language • give examples • put emphasis on • use stylistic devices such as …

3 Viewing Analyse the way Chu's assessments are presented and what function the various visual elements of the video have.

Text 4/5

▶ Getting started

Beyond the text

4 You choose | Writing Work on task **a** or **b**.

a Intercultural communication While Germany tends to be sceptical of nuclear energy, other countries are relying on nuclear power in order to achieve carbon-free energy production. Sometimes these different approaches are discussed in terms of underlying cultural differences: technophobia vs. optimism, 'German Angst' vs. confidence and pragmatism – perhaps this is what it's really about?
An exchange student from the U.S. asks you about the prevalent view held by Germans and about your personal opinion. Write an email in response.

b Imagine the region you live in is very economically dependent on the coal industry. Climate activists have been demanding an immediate end to this industry. The jobs of some of your family members might be threatened.
Write a message in an online forum, stating your point of view.

Text 5

▶ More info

Green city Singapore   Amy Kolczak

- Look at the photograph of the Gardens by the Bay, a public park in Singapore, and describe what you see.

A thriving and growing metropolis, the city state of Singapore has only limited space – a dilemma and not the best precondition for being a 'green city', one might think. The following interview with urban developer Cheong Koon Hean looks at the city's innovative approach towards more sustainability.

Annotations
1 **make good on sth.** fulfil sth.
2 **launch sth.** start sth.
6 **verdant** fresh and green
7 **sustainable** environment-friendly

Singapore calls itself the Garden City, and it's making good on that promise.

Singapore's meteoric economic rise launched a landscape of towering architecture in the compact city-state, but as the metropolis continues to grow, urban planners are weaving nature throughout – and even into its heights. New developments
5 must include plant life, in the form of green roofs, cascading vertical gardens, and verdant walls. [...]

Much of that vision to keep Singapore both sustainable and livable stems from Cheong Koon Hean, the first woman to lead Singapore's urban development agency. [...] *National Geographic* spoke to her about Singapore's unique brand of
10 building – and how one day it may even take the city underground.

Saving the Planet – Our Future at Risk

What distinguishes Singapore as an urban area?
Singapore is both a country and a city – an island about half the size of metropolitan London. But compactness has its advantages: One can take a morning dip in the ocean and then hop on a train to work.

Singapore is truly cosmopolitan, and we've managed to preserve our cultural – Chinese, Indian, and Malay – and architectural legacy through a heritage conservation program. It is a merger of old and new, a mix of the East and West. These are the beautiful contradictions that make Singapore a richly diverse city.

How has Singapore transformed during your 35-year career?
When Singapore became independent in 1965, we were a city filled with slums, choked with congestion, where rivers became open sewers, and we were struggling to find decent jobs for our people. We had limited land and no natural resources. In the short span of 50 years, we have built a clean, modern metropolis with a diversified economy and reliable infrastructure. Our public housing program has transformed us from a nation of squatters to a nation of homeowners: More than 90 percent of our people own their homes, one of the highest home-ownership rates in the world.

Could you describe the initiative to expand the city's green space?
Through an incentive program, we replace greenery lost on the ground from development with greenery in the sky through high-rise terraces and gardens. This adds another layer of space for recreation and gathering. In Marina Bay, all developments comply with a 100 percent greenery replacement policy. The Pinnacle@Duxton, the tallest public housing development in the world, has seven 50-story buildings connected by gardens on the 26th and 50th floors. You can even jog around a track on these levels, which are also equipped with exercise stations.

You're aiming to create a model of 'livable density'. Can you define that?
Given our land constraints, Singapore has no choice but to adopt high-density development. At its essence, livable density is about creating quality of life despite that density. It's about opportunity, variety, and convenience: More jobs result from the synergy of having so many talented people come together. We offer proximity to shops, schools, entertainment, healthcare, and the outdoors. Affordable public rail networks reduce traffic congestion. Livable density also means that we prioritize parks and recreation facilities. Innovative design can reduce that feeling of density by creating the illusion of space using 'green' and 'blue' elements. [...]

Looking ahead, what will Singapore be like in 2030?
Buildings will be green – a major target is to have 80 percent achieve an environmental performance rating called Green Mark by 2030, in order to reduce energy use and carbon emissions. New solutions will support the urban lifestyle: More people will be based in Smart Work Centres – shared work space for employees from different companies – near their homes, reducing the need to travel, improving productivity, and enhancing work-life balance. People will be empowered in new ways with technology – the elderly can be better looked after in their homes with 'tele-medicine'. Technology will also allow us to tap underground and cavern spaces to supplement our limited land. Our urban planners are endeavouring to develop a 3-D masterplan of underground Singapore. [...]

From: 'This City Aims to Be the World's Greenest', www.nationalgeographic.com, 28 February 2017

Info

Situated at the southern end of the Malay Peninsula in Southeast Asia, the **Republic of Singapore** is an island country and a city-state with a population of about 5.8 million. The city is commonly known as 'Garden City' because of its many green spaces and high standard of living. While there is little primary rainforest left in Singapore, there are more than 300 parks and four nature reserves.

Annotations
15 **cosmopolitan** containing people from many different countries and cultural backgrounds
16 **legacy** [ˈlegəsi] inheritance, tradition
16 **heritage** history, buildings, traditions etc. handed down by previous generations
17 **merger** combination
21 **congestion** state of being full of traffic
21 **sewers** waste water and human waste
25 **squatter** person living illegally in sb. else's house or on sb. else's land
33 **public housing** low-cost housing
40 **synergy** positive result of two or more factors (or people) working together instead of separately
51 **enhance sth.** make sth. even better, further improve sth.
53 **tap sth.** make use of a resource that already exists

Text 5/6

▶ Check

Comprehension

1 Complete the following sentences using information from the text:
   1 Singapore is a diverse city – it is a mixture of …
   2 In 1965 the city was …, and 50 years later it is …
   3 In order to expand the city's green space …
   4 'Livable density' is about …
   5 In 2030, Singapore will be …

Analysis

▶ Support p. 31

2 Work on either **a** or **b**.
   a Examine how the text uses *contrast to characterize Singapore.
   b **Challenge** Analyse the means the text employs to present Singapore as a model city.

Language awareness

▶ More language

3 In the text, Cheong's answers to the interview question are given in direct speech.
   a Summarize Cheong's answer to *one* of the interview questions, using indirect speech to report what she says.
   b Assess how the use of indirect speech changes the effect on the reader.

Beyond the text

4 **You choose** Work on either task **a** or **b**.
   a **Writing** Research other 'green cities' (e.g. Vienna, Munich, São Paulo, Madrid, Copenhagen). Write an entry for the city's website summarizing what the city has done to make life more enjoyable and more sustainable.
   b **Speaking** Collect ideas on how to make your own city a greener place to live. Discuss your ideas with a partner.

Text 6

▶ More info

What shall we eat?   Jonathan Safran Foer

- Conduct a survey on eating habits in your class: How many of you follow a special diet (e.g. halal, vegan, vegetarian, …)? Present your results in a chart and discuss them.

In his book We Are the Weather – Saving the Planet Begins at Breakfast *(2019), acclaimed U.S. author Jonathan Safran Foer (born 1977) offers an apparently simple solution to the climate crisis: We can save the planet by changing our everyday eating habits. However, Foer also makes it clear just how difficult it is to do this. The following excerpt is an internal dialogue of the author with himself – a 'dispute of the soul', as he calls it.*

[...] *So you're ... not hopeful?*
I'm not. I know too many smart and caring people – not advocacy narcissists, but good people who give their time, money, and energy to improve the world – who would never change how they eat, no matter how persuaded they were to do so.

These smart and caring people, how would they explain their unwillingness to eat differently?
They would never be asked to.

If they were?
They might say that animal agriculture is a system with serious flaws, but people have to eat, and animal products are cheaper now than they have ever been before.

And how would you respond to that?
I would say we have to eat, but we don't have to eat animal products – we are certainly healthier when plants make up the majority of our diet – and we clearly don't have to eat them in the historically unprecedented quantities that we currently do. But it's true that this is an issue of economic justice. We should talk about it as one, rather than use inequality as a way to avoid talking about inequality.

The richest 10 percent of the global population is responsible for half the carbon emissions; the poorest half is responsible for 10 percent. And those who are the least responsible for global warming are often the ones most punished by it. Consider Bangladesh, the country widely considered to be most vulnerable to climate change. An estimated six million Bangladeshis have already been displaced by environmental disasters like storm surges, tropical cyclones, droughts, and flooding, with millions more projected to become displaced in the coming years. Anticipated sea-level rises could submerge about one-third of the country, uprooting twenty-five to thirty million people.

It would be easy to hear that figure and not feel it. Every year, the *World Happiness Report* ranks the top fifty happiest countries in the world on the basis of how respondents score their lives, from 'the best possible life' to 'the worst possible life'. In 2018, it ranked Finland, Norway, and Denmark as the three happiest countries in the world. When the rankings were released, they clogged NPR for a couple of days, and seemed to come up in every conversation. The combined population of Finland, Norway, and Denmark is approximately half of the number of anticipated Bangladeshi climate refugees. But those thirty million Bangladeshis who are threatened with the worst possible lives don't make for good radio.

Bangladesh has one of the smallest carbon footprints in the world, meaning it is least accountable for the damage that most afflicts it. The average Bangladeshi is responsible for 0.29 metric tons of CO_2 emissions per year, while the average Finn is responsible for about 38 times that: 11.15 metric tons. Bangladesh also happens to be one of the world's most vegetarian countries, where the average person consumes about nine pounds of meat per year. In 2018, the average Finn happily consumed that amount every eighteen days – and that doesn't include seafood.

Millions of Bangladeshis are paying for a resource-opulent lifestyle that they have never themselves enjoyed. Imagine if you had never touched a cigarette in your life

Annotations
2 **advocacy narcissist** [ˈædvəkəsi ˈnɑːsɪsɪst] self-admiring person who loves giving advice to other people
9 **flaw** defect, fault, weakness
24 **submerge sb./sth.** put sb./sth. under the surface of water
24 **uproot sb.** make sb. leave the place where they have lived for a long time
30 **clog sth.** (here) fill sth. up almost entirely
30 **NPR = National Public Radio** U.S. public radio station
36 **be accountable for sth.** be responsible for sth.

Text 6

Annotations
49 **obese** very overweight
49 **stunted** not having grown or developed as much as it should have
50 **malnutrition** *Mangelernährung*
59 **rapporteur** person chosen by an organization to investigate a particular question and report on it
60 **funnel sth.** (here) move sth. from one place to another

but were forced to absorb the health tolls of a chain-smoker on the other side of the planet. Imagine if the smoker remained healthy and at the top of the happiness chart – smoking more cigarettes with each passing year, satisfying his addiction – while you suffered lung cancer.

Worldwide, more than 800 million people are underfed, and nearly 650 million are obese. More than 150 million children under the age of five are physically stunted because of malnutrition. That's another figure that demands a pause. Imagine if everyone living in the United Kingdom and France were under five years old and without enough food to grow properly. Three million children under the age of five die of malnutrition *every year*. One and a half million children died in the Holocaust.

Land that could feed hungry populations is instead reserved for livestock that will feed overfed populations. When we think about food waste, we need to stop imagining half-eaten meals and instead focus on the waste involved in bringing food to the plate. It can require as many as twenty-six calories fed to an animal to produce just one calorie of meat. The UN's former special rapporteur on the right to food, Jean Ziegler, wrote that funnelling one hundred million tons of grain and corn to biofuels is 'a crime against humanity' in a world where almost a billion people are starving. We might call that crime 'manslaughter'. What he didn't mention is that every year, animal agriculture funnels more than seven times that amount of grain and corn – enough to feed every hungry person on the planet – to animals for affluent people to eat. We might call that crime 'genocide'.

So, no, factory farming does not 'feed the world'. Factory farming starves the world as it destroys it. […]

From: We Are the Weather – Saving the World Begins at Breakfast, *2019*

Comprehension

1 Outline the author's view on the connection between our eating habits and the climate.

Analysis

2 Analyse the way Foer tries to convince the reader of his position.

Language awareness

3 At several points, Foer asks his readers to imagine a particular fact or situation (cf. ll. 43–47, 50–52).
   a Explain the grammatical structure used in each case.
   b Outline what function these 'thought experiments' have in the context of Foer's line of argument.
   c Think of other such imagined situations that might be used to further support Foer's arguments. Start like this: 'Imagine if …'

Text 6/7

Beyond the text

4 a Explain the infographic on the right. Point out which part of Safran Foer's argument it supports and what facts not mentioned by Foer it adds to the debate.
   b Work with a partner. Discuss what kind of presentation of facts and arguments you find more persuasive: an *argumentative text or an infographic?

5 Now that you have read Foer's text, do a quick update of your previous class survey. Are the results any different? If so, how?

6 `You choose` Work on either **a** or **b**.
   a `Speaking` Get together in groups of four. Each of you gets a role card. Prepare for a discussion about the impact of eating habits on our climate.
   b `Writing` Write a blog post in which you respond to Safran Foer.

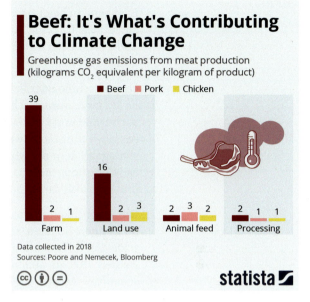

Text 7

Sustainability at German schools   Anima Müller

- Talk about your school, youth club or sports club: Are there any projects to protect the environment or raise environmental awareness? Exchange your knowledge.

The following excerpt from a German newspaper article presents an initiative at the Ecolea, a school in Rostock, where social workers, teachers and students all work together to attempt to reduce the school's CO_2 emissions and promote sustainability projects.

[…] Grit Weickert, Sozialarbeiterin des internationalen Gymnasiums, sah in dem plastikfreien Kiosk Potenzial und plante zwei groß angelegte Projekte: eins zum ökologischen Fußabdruck der Schule, das andere zum Thema Mülltrennung. Nun suchen 15 Schüler*innen ein Jahr lang „Tatorte" an der Schule, an denen sich der
5 CO_2-Verbrauch drücken lässt. Und die 5. Klassen untersuchen über einen Zeitraum von zwei Jahren das Abfallsystem der Schule und Müllprobleme weltweit.

Dabei lernen sie unter anderem, in welche Tonne gebrauchte Taschentücher kommen (richtige Antwort: Restmüll). Oder wie viel Plastik Menschen in Deutschland im Jahr verbrauchen (rund 38 Kilo pro Person). „Das hat mich selbst ganz schön
10 überrascht", sagt Grit Weickert. Es ist das erste Mal, dass die Schule längerfristige Nachhaltigkeitsprojekte startet, für die Fördermittel beantragt und zum Teil schon bewilligt wurden.

So wie die Ecolea Rostock engagieren sich mittlerweile viele Schulen im Bereich Nachhaltigkeit. In Deutschland entstehen immer neue Auszeichnungen, die ihr Engagement belohnen – und immer mehr Schulen zeigen Interesse. Ob sich auch die Ecolea für eine Auszeichnung bewerben soll, hat Weickert noch nicht abschließend entschieden – sie könnte es sich aber gut vorstellen. „Ich bin der Meinung, dass man erst ein paar Jahre Erfahrung sammeln muss", sagt sie.

Umweltschule oder lieber Klimaschule?

Es sei zwar immer schön für eine Schule, Zertifikate zu haben. „Das muss aber auch Hand und Fuß haben." Denn Weickert und ihre Kolleg*innen planen einiges, das noch umgesetzt werden soll: Teil des Müllprojekts der 5. Klassen ist ein Projekttag, an dem der Müllverbrauch der eigenen Schule bestimmt wird. Dann soll es Workshops geben, Exkursionen zum regionalen Entsorgungsunternehmen und eine Müllsammelaktion im Mündungsgebiet der Warnow.

Die Möglichkeiten für eine Bewerbung sind in Deutschland jedenfalls zahlreich. So können Schulen Teil des Unesco-Netzwerks werden oder sich um ein Fairtrade-Siegel bemühen, „Verbraucherschule" oder „Umweltschule in Europa" werden. Neben anderen, deutschlandweiten Preisen gibt es eine kaum überschaubare Anzahl regionaler Auszeichnungen. Die größeren, auf die sich zum Teil mehrere hundert Schulen bewerben, werden meist durch die jeweiligen Kultus- und Umweltministerien vergeben. Sie heißen sehr ähnlich: „Schule der Zukunft" in Nordrhein-Westfalen, „Umweltschule" in Hessen, „Zukunftsschule" in Schleswig-Holstein oder „Nachhaltige Schule" in Rheinland-Pfalz. [...]

1.500 Umweltschulen in Deutschland

„Mein Ziel ist es, ein einigermaßen homogenes Programm für Deutschland zu schaffen", sagt Robert Lorenz, der die Auszeichnung „Umweltschule für Europa – internationale Nachhaltigkeitsschule" in Deutschland koordiniert. Das Projekt der Deutschen Gesellschaft für Umwelterziehung (DGU) ist das größte Nachhaltigkeitsnetzwerk für Schulen im Land. Es entstand im Jahr 1994 mit acht Schulen in Hamburg, mittlerweile sind deutschlandweit etwa 1.500 dabei. Verliehen wird die Auszeichnung unter dem englischen Titel „Eco School" auch in knapp 70 anderen Ländern, organisiert durch den internationalen Dachverband Foundation for Environmental Education (FEE). [...]

Für die Schulen sind die Label wichtig, glaubt auch Wissenschaftlerin Ingrid Hemmer. Sie stiften Zusammenhalt, können eine Plattform geben, um die Bemühungen engagierter Lehrkräfte und Schüler*innen zu würdigen. Sie bieten Schulen die Möglichkeit, sich mit anderen über ihre Projekte auszutauschen. Nicht zuletzt wirken sie sich auch positiv auf die Außenwahrnehmung aus [...]

Ein Musterbeispiel einer „Umweltschule" ist das Dossenberger Gymnasium im schwäbischen Günzburg. In Bayern tragen besonders viele Schulen die Auszeichnung, etwa zwölf Prozent haben sich laut bayerischer Landeskoordination der DGU mittlerweile beworben, Tendenz steigend. In diesem Jahr waren es 600 Schulen. Seit zwölf Jahren trägt das Dossenberger Gymnasium den Titel, zu großen Teilen ein Verdienst von Kunstlehrerin Birgit Rembold. [...]

Über die Jahre hinweg haben sie und ihre Kolleg*innen das Gymnasium in einen kleinen Nachhaltigkeitskosmos verwandelt: Nach den Sommerferien startet eine „Umweltklasse", die zweimal pro Woche im Fach Umweltbildung unterrichtet wird. Am „Zukunftstag" wird ein umweltfreundliches Schulfest gefeiert, längst gibt es nur noch Recyclingpapier. Zum Ende eines Schuljahres beschäftigt sich jede Klassenstufe mit Umweltthemen: Die 7. Klassen arbeiten zu den Themen Wiese und Insekten und besuchen das schuleigene Insektenhotel. „Vom Imker gibt es dann eine Honigsemmel", sagt Rembold. [...]

From: "Eine Honigsemmel vom Imker", taz.de, 29 August 2020

▶ Getting started

1 Mediating Your school has just become an 'eco-school'. For its bilingual website write a short article (in English) on the situation of eco-school programs in Germany.

▶ SF 47: Mediating from German into English, Student's book p. 332

Chapter task

After dealing with various ideas for a sustainable future, you are planning an ecoproject in your community, e.g. in your school, neighbourhood or sports club, as your answer to this chapter's guiding question 'There is no Planet B – how can we save Planet A?'.

Collect ideas on your project and prepare a presentation to the class to try to persuade other students to join your group.

1 Work in groups of three or four students.

  a Discuss the following aspects of your project and take notes.
  - **Ideas:** Collect ideas: a meat-free day in your school canteen, collecting rubbish in your local park, saving rain water to water your football field in summer, …
  - **Steps:** Make a list of the steps you need to follow to realize your project. List all the material you may need. If necessary, think about possible sponsors or ways to raise money.
  - **Partners:** Think about what kind of help you might need to realize your project and who you might contact – classmates, the caretaker of your school, neighbours, the mayor of your town, …
  - **Roles:** Think about everything that needs to be done and assign each task to one group member. Who is responsible for networking with other organizations, who will take photographs or make videos, who does the writing, who is responsible for time management?
  - **Promotion:** How will you raise public awareness and make your project heard and seen by others? Are you going to use social media, write a newspaper article or a blog, report on your work in a podcast?

  b Prepare a presentation on your project to persuade students to join your group.

▶ Getting started

2 Speaking Give your presentation in front of the class.

3 Take a vote: Which project group would most students want to join?

▶ SF 41: Giving a presentation, Student's book p. 321

Support and Partner B

Text 1

▶ p. 10

Climate activism

Partner B
Prince Ea is a U.S. spoken-word artist and motivational speaker whose online videos have received over 330 million views. Read the following text.

Man vs Earth   Prince Ea

Annotations
7 **drumroll**
   Trommelwirbel
19 **quest** search
20 **neglect sb./sth.** ignore sb./sth.

Fun fact: planet Earth is 4.5 billion years old.
Mankind? About 140,000 years old.
Let me put that in perspective:
If you condense the Earth's lifespan into 24 hours,
5 that's one full day,
then we have been here on this planet for …
… drumroll please …
… three seconds.
Three seconds, and look what we've done.
10 We have modestly named ourselves 'homo sapiens'
meaning 'wise man', but is man really so wise?
Smart, yes, and it's good to be smart,
but not too smart for your own good.
Yes, we have split the atom.
15 Yes, we build clever machines that
navigate the universe in search of new homes.
But at the same time,
those atoms we split created nuclear warfare.
In our quest to explore the galaxy,
20 rejects and neglects the home that we have here now.
So no, that cannot be wisdom.
Wisdom is different.
While intelligence speaks, wisdom listens.
And we willingly covered our ears
25 to mother nature's screams …
and closed our eyes to all of her 'Help Wanted' signs.
Wisdom knows that every action
has an equal and opposite reaction.
So if we were wise, we would not be shocked
30 when we see storms that are stronger than ever before.
Or more drought, hurricanes and wildfire than ever before.
Because there's more pollution than ever before.
More carbon, more trees cut down than ever before
at a record pace.

Support and Partner B

35 We have increased the extinction of animals
    by one thousand times the normal rate.
    What a feat.
    In the next ten to a hundred years,
    every beloved animal character
40 in every children's book
    is predicted to go extinct.
    Lions? Gone.
    Rhinos? Gone.
    Tiger? Gorilla? Elephant? Polar bear?
45 Gone. In three seconds.
    Species that have been here longer than us
    will be gone because of us in these three seconds.
    In an existence shorter than a Vine video,
    we turned the circle of life
50 into our own personal conveyor belt.
    Somebody, anybody, help!
    We were given so much.
    The only planet in this solar system with life.
    I mean, we are one in a million –
55 no, actually, scientifically,
    we are one in a billion trillion trillion.
    That's a 1 followed by 33 zeros.
    And I don't wanna get too spiritual,
    but how are we not a miracle?
60 We are perfectly positioned to the sun so we don't burn,
    but not too distant so we don't turn to ice.
    Goldilocks said it best: We are just right.
    This paradise.
    Where we are given medicine from trees,
65 not coincidentally.
    But because like the song says:
    We are family. Literally.
    Everything. Every species is connected genetically,
    from the sunflower to the sunfish.
70 And this is what we must recognize before it's too late.
    Because the real crisis is not global warming,
    environmental destruction, or animal agriculture.
    It is us.
    These problems are symptoms of us.
75 Byproducts of us.
    Our inner reflection,
    loss of connection has created this misdirection.
    We have forgotten that everything contributes
    to the perfection of Mother Nature.
80 Corporations keep us unaware and disconnected,
    but they have underestimated our strength.
    Contrary to popular belief
    millions are waking up out of their sleep.

Annotations
37 **feat** great achievement
48 **Vine** online portal for uploading videos of max. 6 seconds in length (2012–2017)
50 **conveyor belt** continuously moving band for transporting goods, e.g. in a factory
62 **Goldilocks** one of the characters in the fairy tale 'Goldilocks and the Three Bears'
65 **coincidentally** by chance

Support and Partner B

Annotations
87 **wicked** [ˈwɪkɪd] mean, immoral
87 **loony** (infml) crazy, demented

       Seeing our home being taken
85 right up from under our feet.
       We cannot allow our history to be
       written by the wicked, greedy, and loony.
       It is our duty to protect Mother Nature
       from those who refuse to see her beauty.
90 Call me crazy,
       but I believe we should have the right
       to eat food that's safe,
       With ingredients we can pronounce,
       drink water that is clean,
95 marvel at trees, breathe air free of toxins.
       These are natural rights,
       not things that can be bargained for in Congress.
       See they want you to feel powerless.
       But it has been said that something
100 as small as the flutter of a butterfly's wing
       can cause a typhoon halfway around the world.
       Well, when enough people come together,
       we too will make waves.
       And wash the world into a new era
105 filled with love and connection.
       Freedom for all without oppression.
       But it is up to you.
       Yes, you watching this behind this screen
       to make the effort.
110 Because time is of the essence.
       And only together can we make it
       to the fourth second.

From: Prince Ea

Comprehension

1 For your partner, summarize the main message of the text you have read.

Analysis

▶ Support p. 31

2 **a** Analyse the *stylistic devices used in your text in order to convince the audience.
     b Choose two examples and present them to your partner.
Now go back to task 3 on p. 11.

Support and Partner B

2 Support ▶ Check

Greta Thunberg
Name the *stylistic device in each of these Greta Thunberg quotes:
- 'I shouldn't be standing here. I should be back in school […]' (ll. 1–2)
- 'science has been crystal clear' (l. 9)

Find a quote from the text matching the following stylistic devices
- *anaphora
- *repetition
- *metaphor

Now go back to your original task on p. 11.

Prince Ea
Name the *stylistic device for each of these Prince Ea quotes:
- 'but is man really so wise?' (l. 11)
- 'while intelligence speaks, wisdom listens' (l. 23)
- 'storms stronger than ever before' (l. 30)

Find a quote from the text matching the following stylistic devices
- *repetition
- *personification
- *enumeration

Now go back to your original task.

Text 3

After the storm

4 Support ▶ p. 17

Novelists often use descriptions of nature, the weather, or landscapes and surroundings to mirror a character's inner life. Explain the connection between the devastation left behind by Hurricane Katrina and Esch's state of mind.
Now go back to task 4.

Text 5

Green city Singapore

2 Support ▶ p. 22

Consider the following phrases:
- 'a country and a city' (l. 12)
- 'old and new' (l. 17)
- 'a mix of the East and West' (l. 17)
- 'a city filled with slums' (l. 20)
- 'clean, modern metropolis' (l. 23).

Now go back to task 4.

Acknowledgements

Cover
Shutterstock.com/DisobeyArt

Photos
pp. 6/7: Shutterstock.com/ParabolStudio; **p. 9** top: Shutterstock.com/marekuliasz, bottom: Shutterstock.com/DisobeyArt; **p. 10**: Shutterstock.com/robertindiana; **p. 13**: Shutterstock.com/graficriver_icons_logo; **p. 14**: Shutterstock.com/Dmitry Demidovich; **p. 16**: Shutterstock.com/Alexander Remy Levine; **p. 18**: Brown, Don. Drowned City: Hurricane Katrina and New Orleans. Brown - Houghton Mifflin, 2017; **p. 20**: Shutterstock.com/Tobias Kaeter; **p. 22**: Shutterstock.com/MOLPIX; **p. 25**: Sources: Poore and Nemcek, Bloomberg. Data collected in 2018. https://www.statista.com/chart/22450/meat-production-and-climate-change/© Statista 2021

Texts
pp. 10–11: Thunberg, Greta. *No One Is Too Small to Make a Difference*. Penguin, 2019; **pp. 11–13**: Weston, Phoebe. "Top scientists warn of 'ghastly future of mass extinction' and climate disruption". *theguardian.com*, 13 Jan 2021, https://www.theguardian.com/environment/2021/jan/13/top-scientists-warn-of-ghastly-future-of-mass-extinction-and-climate-disruption-aoe (accessed 16.12.2021); **pp. 15–17**: Ward, Jesmyn. *Salvage the Bones*. London, Bloomsbury Publishing, 2011, pp. 240-243; **pp. 20–21**: Hean, Cheong Koon. Interview by Amy Kolczak. "This City Aims to Be the World's Greenest." *National Geographic*, 28 Feb. 2017, www.nationalgeographic.com/environment/article/green-urban-landscape-cities-Singapore (accessed 5 Aug. 2021); **pp. 22–24**: Foer, Jonathan Safran. *We Are the Weather - Saving the World Begins at Breakfast*. London, Penguin, 2019, pp. 163-166; **pp. 25–27**: Müller, Anima. „Eine Honigsemmel vom Imker", *taz.de*, 29.8.2020, https://taz.de/Umweltschutz-an-Schulen-in-Deutschland/!5704361/; **pp. 28–30**: Prince EA, "Man vs. Earth". *Genius*, https://genius.com/Prince-ea-man-vs-earth-annotated

Topics in Context

Context

Being Young – Joys and Challenges

Themenheft

Cornelsen

Context

Being Young – Joys and Challenges

Im Auftrag des Verlages herausgegeben von
Dr. Annette Leithner-Brauns, Dresden

Erarbeitet von
Martina Baasner, Berlin; Irene Bartscherer, Bonn; Lisa Braun, Meppen; Dr. Sabine Buchholz, Hürth; Wiebke Bettina Dietrich, Göttingen; Sylvia Loh, Esslingen; Benjamin Lorenz, Bensheim; Dr. Paul Maloney, Hildesheim; Dr. Pascal Ohlmann, Tholey; Birgit Ohmsieder, Berlin; Dr. Andreas Sedlatschek, Esslingen; Veronika Walther, Rudolstadt

In Zusammenarbeit mit der Englischredaktion
Dr. Marion Kiffe (Koordinierende Redakteurin), Dr. Christiane Kallenbach (Projektleitung), Aryane Beaudoin, Dr. Jan Dreßler, Hartmut Tschepe, Dr. Christian von Raumer, Freya Wurm *unter Mitwirkung von* Janan Barksdale, Irja Fröhling, Katrin Gütermann, Anne Müller, Neil Porter, Evelyn Sternad, Mai Weber

Beratende Mitwirkung
Ramin Azadian, Berlin; Heiko Benzin, Neustrelitz; Sabine Otto, Halle (Saale)

Layoutkonzept
Klein & Halm, Berlin

Layout und technische Umsetzung
Straive
designcollective, Berlin

Umschlaggestaltung
Rosendahl, Berlin

Lizenzmanagement
Britta Bensmann

Weitere Bestandteile des Lehrwerks
- **Schulbuch** (print und als E-Book)
- **E-Books** (in zwei Varianten: 1. alle *Topics in Context* bzw. 2. Schulbuch und *Topics in Context*)
- *Lehrkräftefassung des Schulbuchs* (im Unterrichtsmanager)
- *Handreichungen für den Unterricht* (print und im Unterrichtsmanager)
- **Workbook** (print)
- *Unterrichtsmanager*
- *Vorschläge zur Leistungsmessung* (digital)
- *Cornelsen Lernen App*

---

www.cornelsen.de

Die Webseiten Dritter, deren Internetadressen in diesem Lehrwerk angegeben sind, wurden vor Drucklegung sorgfältig geprüft. Der Verlag übernimmt keine Gewähr für die Aktualität und den Inhalt dieser Seiten oder solcher, die mit ihnen verlinkt sind.

1. Auflage, 1. Druck 2022

Alle Drucke dieser Auflage sind inhaltlich unverändert und können im Unterricht nebeneinander verwendet werden.

© 2022 Cornelsen Verlag GmbH, Berlin

Das Werk und seine Teile sind urheberrechtlich geschützt. Jede Nutzung in anderen als den gesetzlich zugelassenen Fällen bedarf der vorherigen schriftlichen Einwilligung des Verlages. Hinweis zu §§ 60 a, 60 b UrhG: Weder das Werk noch seine Teile dürfen ohne eine solche Einwilligung an Schulen oder in Unterrichts- und Lehrmedien (§ 60 b Abs. 3 UrhG) vervielfältigt, insbesondere kopiert oder eingescannt, verbreitet oder in ein Netzwerk eingestellt oder sonst öffentlich zugänglich gemacht oder wiedergegeben werden. Dies gilt auch für Intranets von Schulen.

Druck: H. Heenemann, Berlin

ISBN 978-3-06-036525-8

PEFC zertifiziert
Dieses Produkt stammt aus nachhaltig bewirtschafteten Wäldern und kontrollierten Quellen.
www.pefc.de
PEFC/04-31-1156

Contents

Title	Topic	Text type / media	Skills	Page
Lead-in				4
Words in Context: Adolescence – an in-between phase	*Youth* as a social construct Characteristics of adolescence	Informative text		6
Text 1: Youth cultures throughout history	Youth cultures of the past New identities	Audio file 🔊	Listening Writing Speaking	8
Info box: Between childhood and adulthood: youth culture	*Youth* as a social construct	Informative text		9
Text 2: Generation Z – are the kids alright? *Nosheen Iqbal*	Lifestyle and values of Generation Z	Newspaper article	Writing	10
Text 3: Is 'OK, Boomer' ok, Boomer? *Rezo*	Generation conflicts Generation Z and Baby Boomers	Newspaper article	Mediating	13
Text 4: Someone desirable *Nick Hornby*	Love Identity	Novel extract	Speaking Writing	14
Text 5: Beauty ideals and social media	Different ideals in contemporary society Challenges of youth	Video ▶	Viewing Speaking Writing	18
Text 6: Art in Context: 'The fountain of youth' *Lucas Cranach the Elder*	Approaching art The connection between youth and beauty	Painting	Analysing a painting	19
Text 7: Eternal youth? 'Sonnet XVII' *William Shakespeare* 'Forever young' *Bob Dylan*	Preserving youth Love Beauty	Sonnet Song	Analysing a song/ sonnet Writing	20
Text 8: Lifelong lessons? *Emma Jacobs*	Gap years Seeking meaning in life Exploring the world	Newspaper article	Speaking Writing	21
Text 9: Routes into work *Tess Reidy*	Choosing a career Bridging the gap	Newspaper article	Speaking Intercultural communication	23
Chapter Task: A message to myself			Writing	25
Support and Partner B				26
Acknowledgements				28
Abbreviations			inner front cover	

Being Young – Joys and Challenges

1. **a** Look at the pictures. Decide which pictures best represent your ideas of being young.
   b Discuss your choices with a partner and agree on three pictures that both of you consider characteristic of youth. Add convincing *headings for them.

2. **a** Copy and fill in the table below. Refer to the pictures first, then add ideas of your own.

Present joys	Present worries	Future hopes	Future fears
…	…	…	…

   b Add to your table as you work on the texts in this chapter.

3. *__Quick write:__ Look at the Chapter map on the right. Refer to the topics listed there and do a quick write on your initial spontaneous reaction to the guiding question.

Chapter map

youth culture(s) · Generation Z · relationships

Youth issues: Who am I, and who will I be?

Chapter task: a message ✓

eternal youth · beauty ideals · life after school · social media

Words in Context

Adolescence: an in-between phase

Youth – or adolescence – is the stage of life between childhood and adulthood. During this phase, adolescents undergo physiological and psychological changes that eventually prepare them for their adult lives, with all the legal and social issues this implies.

Youth and society

5 It may seem that 'youth' is a universal category that has always existed in all cultures around the world. But this is not the case: In many cultures, adolescents used to be or still are treated like grown-ups, leaving no room for the lifestyles and experiences usually attributed to young people.

In most modern Western societies, however, 'youth' does exist as an independent
10 phase in a person's life. Here, adolescence is a phase in which young people are allowed to experiment with and explore different possibilities before eventually making a commitment e.g. to values, a profession, or a partner. Birthday parties, school proms or a driver's licence can be considered modern rites of passage that mark young people's coming of age and celebrate their independence.

15 While their peer group becomes more important for young people, their relationship with their parents may be affected by conflict and distancing. Such conflicts between members of different generations, the so-called 'generation gap', often result from contrasting perspectives on life. Types of behaviour that are considered rebellious or nonconformist by the older generation may evolve into distinctive forms of youth cul-
20 ture that show their creative potential by setting trends or influencing public discourse.

Challenges

Despite the liberties of youth, coming of age is often experienced as a period of inner turmoil – or 'teenage angst'. Factors such as uncertainty about their appearance, peer
25 pressure and fear of social exclusion may lead young people to greater risk-taking e.g. by experimenting with drugs or in their sexual activities. Their need to seek praise, especially in social media, can turn into an obsession with self-optimization. This may lead to self-doubt and low self-esteem rather than to body positivity. Ongoing frustration with unattainable ideals may eventually result in serious health conditions such
30 as depression or eating disorders.

Future plans

Finishing school is undoubtedly a major milestone on the path to adulthood. Depending on their qualifications and interests, school leavers can enrol at university or a further education college, become an apprentice or start vocational training. Others
35 take up an internship before they commit to a career path, or they take a gap year in order to travel, engage in voluntary work or simply to find out where their interests lie. Whatever decisions young people make, these may or may not turn out to be the right ones for their future. But it is always possible to make new decisions and head in a different direction.

Being Young – Joys and Challenges

Words in Context

1 Words words words

Work in groups of three, with each person concentrating on one of the three major paragraphs in the text.
  a Prepare a short oral summary of your paragraph. From the highlighted words in the text choose three that you find central to your paragraph and use them in your summary.
  b Present your summaries to each other. While listening, note down useful words.
  c Compare your lists of words and add words from your partners' lists to yours.
  d Choose three words and explain them to your partners, e.g. by paraphrasing or defining them or by using synonyms or antonyms. Let your partners guess the words.

2 Mind mapping

  a Draw a mind map containing the words from **1**.
  b Go through the text again and add further words to your mind map.

3 Chunk it!

  a In the text, the following words go together with other words to form *chunks. Identify them:
   1 … changes (l. 2)
   2 … perspectives (l. 18)
   3 … praise (l. 26)
   4 … ideals (l. 29)
   5 … internship (l. 35)

  b For each gap in **a** think of at least two more words to form chunks.
  c Look for possible chunks for ten other words from **2**, either in the text or in a dictionary. Add them to your mind map.

▶ Getting started
▶ Check

4 Defining youth

You choose   Work on either task **a** or **b**. Use as many words from tasks **1–3** as you can.
  a Discuss with a partner to what extent the ideas in the text match your own concept of youth.
      ▶ Language help
  b Writing   Write a short definition of the term *adulthood*. It can be serious or funny.

> **Language help**
>
> contrast with sth. • correspond to sth. • contradict sth. • match sth. • doubt sth. • (dis)agree with sth. • object to the idea that … • hold/have a different view / the same view as sb. • be of the same opinion as sb.

Youth issues: Who am I, and who will I be?   **7**

Text 1

Youth cultures throughout history

- Look at the pictures below and say which of them represent the concept of freedom, youthful rebellion and/or nonconformity best.
- Compare your choice with a partner. Confirm or revise your original choice and explain your reasons.

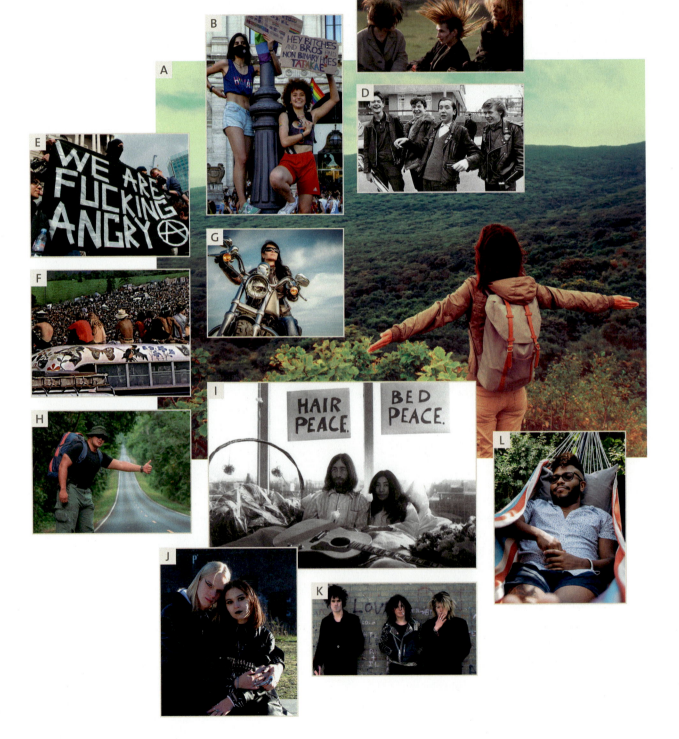

Being Young – Joys and Challenges

Text 1

> **Info**
>
> **Between childhood and adulthood: youth culture**
>
> It may sound surprising that 'youth' as a distinct phase between childhood and adulthood is not universal across all human societies. Where there is no youth culture, children are expected to behave as adults as soon as they are physically and intellec-
> 5 tually able to do so.
>
> Independent youth cultures tend to be a phenomenon of modern industrialized societies, and they are generally believed to have emerged in the 20th century. Sociologists regard compulsory schooling as a major reason for the formation of a youth culture: At school, adolescents mainly interact with other young people,
> 10 which means an independent culture can develop. Adolescents who do not attend school mostly live among grown-ups and tend to adopt adult norms and values.
>
> Youth cultures strive to set themselves apart from the parental generation. Areas in which adolescents differ from their parents can be values and norms, musical
> 15 tastes, clothing styles, interests and even the way they use language: They may use words differently from grown-ups, or use different words altogether.
>
> Youth cultures also tend to diversify, which means that there is not only one, but many youth cultures at any one time. While this diversification may help adolescents find a peer group that suits their personality, it also often leads to animosity
> 20 between youth cultures. For example, in Britain in the 1970s, there were frequent violent clashes between mods and rockers. The 1980s brought about a diversification of youth tribes. Often, depending on their musical preferences, New Romantics, Metal-heads, Yuppies, New-wavers, Rastas existed side by side.
>
> **1** Referring to youth cultures of the past or the present, give examples of how they may differ from that of the older generation in terms of values, clothing and musical tastes.

Comprehension

🔊 **1** **Listening** Listen to three soundbites about youth cultures in the 1970s and 1980s. Make notes on
  1. what mods would wear
  2. what role Jean-Paul Belmondo played for mods
  3. what could happen if you went to a punk concert
  4. how rockers felt when they met mods.

Annotations
run the gauntlet
Spießruten laufen

▶ Check

▶ SF 38: Listening/Viewing for gist and detail, Student's book p. 314

Beyond the text

2 **You choose** Work on either task **a** or **b**.

a **Writing** Write a short *blog post on the advantages and downsides of belonging to a youth culture.

b **Speaking** Do youth cultures still exist today? Give a 2-minute talk.

▶ SF 27: Writing a blog post, Student's book p. 300

Youth issues: Who am I, and who will I be? **9**

Text 2

Generation Z – are the kids alright? Nosheen Iqbal

Info

The Baby Boomers (born 1965–1969)

Generation X (born 1969–1981)

Millennials / Generation Y (born 1982–1995)

Generation Z (born 1996–2015)

Generation Alpha (succeeded Gen Z)

- **Think** What do you associate with being young? Collect at least five ideas. You might think of interests, activities, peer group and social relations, attitudes and style, privileges, challenges etc.

- **Pair** Compare ideas with a partner and agree on five concepts that both of you consider characteristic of your generation.

- **Share** Share ideas with another pair of students and write a portrait of your generation. Reflect on how your views on the guiding question may have changed.

Now read what some British teenagers consider typical of Generation Z.

They drink less, take far fewer drugs, and have made teenage pregnancy a near anomaly. Generation Z – one of several terms used to describe post-millennial youth born after 1996 – prefer juice bars to pub crawls, rank quality family time ahead of sex and prioritise good grades before friendship, 5 at least according to a report published by the British Pregnancy Advisory Service [...].

An onslaught of sneering headlines followed, characterising today's youth as boring, sensible and hopelessly screen-addicted.

So, are the kids all right?

10 'We have so much more to do than [just] drink and take drugs,' says Demi Babalola, a 19-year-old philosophy and sociology student. 'I'm not surprised those [statistics] show that's the case: it makes sense. We have a lot more to distract us now.'

What's her biggest time stealer? 'Social media.' Babalola toggles between Snap-15 chat, Twitter and Instagram, although she rolls her eyes at the mention of Facebook, full as it is of 'older people'.

But it's not just the breadth of entertainment and culture that is so instantly available – and disposable – to Babalola and her peers. There is also a growing feeling that the preoccupations of her parents' generation seem, well, a bit lame.

20 'Going out takes a lot of effort: it's boring, repetitive and expensive,' she says. 'Obviously, I used to go out a lot in my first year [at university], but now we do more kickbacks.'

To the uninitiated, a kickback is the sophisticated Gen Z sweet spot between the lairy house parties of yore – the ones typified by vomit on the parental carpet and a 25 trashing of the family bathroom – and a pre-teen sleepover.

'We hang out, we listen to music, make our own food, and play games,' she says. 'We'll probably organise it a couple of days before.'

Lewis Alley, 14, from Cornwall, agrees. 'We're quite different [from your generation] because there's more stuff to do at each other's houses and we have more 30 technology – like, we have video games.' [...]

The cliche that many young people spend far too much time online, instead of indulging in a romanticised form of rebellion, may have some truth, but as futurologist Rhiannon McGregor points out, Gen Z-ers are more cautious and risk-averse than their parents, partly because that technology exists.

35 'They're aware from an early age of how they're portrayed online and offline, so they curate themselves in a more conservative way,' she says. (In other words, no one wants to be publicly shamed getting messy or being recklessly daft.)

Annotations

2 **anomaly** sth. that is unusual/uncommon
3 **pub crawl** act of visiting several pubs and consuming drinks
7 **onslaught** (here) a rush of messages
7 **sneering** sarcastic
14 **toggle between x and y** (here) switch from one application to another
18 **disposable** not really needed
19 **preoccupation** worry
23 **the uninitiated** (humorous) inexperienced people
23 **sweet spot** (here) optimum combination
24 **lairy** (here) loud and exciting
24 **of yore** (humorous) in the past
32 **indulge in sth.** enjoy sth.
33 **risk-averse** not willing to take risks
36 **curate yourself** (here) present yourself online
37 **daft** (infml) silly

'But they're also more socially aware and see themselves as part of a global community. It's easier to get and feel connected to someone in Africa or Asia and share concerns about climate change, for instance.'
Clara Finnigan, 22, who grew up in Devon and is in her final year at the University of Arts London, points out that one size doesn't fit all. She still goes out, 'often to gay clubs'.
She believes her generation is unfairly judged and that it reports levels of stress and depression that are higher than ever because of the economic and political state of the world it has inherited.

'The whole anxiety of not having stability in your future is something that is definitely very present. I won't probably ever own my own house, unless I get really lucky.' [...] 'I don't expect to have one full-time gig; my career won't be defined by one job. I know I'll have to do stuff I don't enjoy to be able to do passion projects that I do.' [...]
The subjects of Brexit and of dropping out of university to pursue less mind-bogglingly expensive apprenticeships come up a lot. As does a consistent refusal to accept that anyone should be defined by traditional markers of identity. 'We're more inclusive,' says Babalola. 'You can do what you want as long as you don't harm anyone and stay safe. It's about freedom. Previous generations always made distinct separations between being gay or straight.
'I try to avoid labels – being a black girl means society already has certain stereotypes that are expected, like I should be outspoken or "sassy" or loud or like certain music.' Another eyeroll. 'It's restricting.' [...]
While statistics show that smoking, drinking and clubbing may be in decline for today's young people, the health and wellness industry is booming with the same demographic – in part because these young people have had so much information at their disposal. [...] Generation Z-ers will, after all, be living longer and more healthily, and looking better for it.
A report from the Institute of Alcohol Studies suggests that changing demographics also play a part, reporting that 'ethnic minority children ... are less likely to drink, [which] can directly explain a small proportion of the fall in underage drinking' but also that there is evidence these same minority students can also influence their peers. 'Non-Muslim children in schools with a high Muslim population are less likely to drink,' it states.
So what is the new going out? The Generation Z idea of fun that is inexplicable to older adults? [...] Allely and Babalola instantly refer me to Snapchat, where they communicate in a constant group feed with their friends. Broadcasting the minutiae of her day – a good oufit, a trip to Westfield – is as second nature as breathing to Babalola.
'It's kind of documenting your life, but you have an audience and you immediately know who's interacting. I enjoy it – it makes me feel important that 100 people are watching what I'm eating.' [...] And what are Babalola's plans for today? 'My friends and I go out to London, or cycling. We might go to a cute cafe and take pictures.'

From: 'Generation Z: "We have more to do than drink and take drugs"', theguardian.com
21 July 2018

Annotations
50 **anxiety** fearfulness, nervousness
52 **gig** (AE) job
55 **pursue sth.** (here) engage in sth.
56 **mind-boggling** very surprising
56 **apprenticeship** Ausbildung
61 **label** (n) (here) attachment of characteristics to a person or group in order to define them
62 **sassy** (AE infml) bold and lively
64 **be in decline** become less frequent
66 **demographic** (n) section of a society that shares certain features
77 **minutiae** [maɪˈnjuːʃiaɪ] (pl) precise details
78 **Westfield** shopping centre in London

Text 2

Comprehension

1 Point out how Generation Z is described in the report mentioned, by the media and by some of its representatives.

2 Sum up the differences between Generation Z and older generations as presented in the text.

Analysis

▶ SF 17: Reading and understanding non-fictional texts, Student's book p. 285

3 Examine Nosheen Iqbal's attitude towards Generation Z. Consider the language, style and structure of her article.

Language awareness

▶ Getting started

4 This portrayal of Generation Z makes frequent use of colloquial language, especially when somebody is quoted. List five examples and rewrite them in a more formal register.

Beyond the text

▶ Getting started
▶ SF 26: Argumentative writing: discussion and comment, Student's book p. 298
▶ SF 35: Writing a letter to the editor, Student's book, p. 310

5 **You choose** | **Writing** Work on either task **a** or **b**.

a Is today's youth 'boring, sensible and hopelessly screen-addicted' (l. 7)? Write a letter to the editor expressing your view on this quote.

b Leave a comment on the newspaper's website calling for greater tolerance and understanding of Generation Z-ers.

Language help

(fully) agree with … • be of the same opinion as • I think it's true that … • be convinced that … • wonder if you should rather… • Couldn't it be that… • doubt if … • not agree at all • see the point in … • I feel I need to contradict

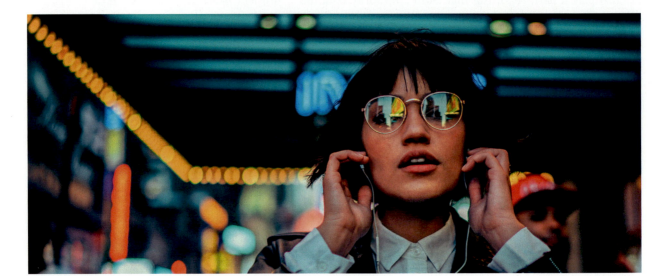

12 Being Young – Joys and Challenges

Text 3

Is 'OK, Boomer' ok, Boomer? Rezo

- Can you think of a typical phrase, greeting or joke used by your generation? What does it mean? Do you use it too?

On the website of the German weekly Die Zeit, *German social media influencer Rezo defends young people using 'OK, boomer' to silence older people who treat them without respect.*

Liebe ZEIT-ONLINE-Leser, heute habe ich gleich zu Beginn mal eine Frage: Wurdet Ihr zwischen 1955 und 1969 geboren, gehört also zu einem der Jahrgänge der deutschen Babyboomergeneration? Dann habe ich für Euch jetzt eine harte Wahrheit: Es ist völlig okay, wenn Leute irrationale und respektlose Statements
5 von Euch mit „OK, Boomer" abqualifizieren. Nicht nur das: Es ist sogar ziemlich heilsam und wichtig, dass Euch das passiert. Denn „OK, Boomer" ist mehr als nachvollziehbar und noch extrem lieb und konstruktiv gegenüber dem, was die mächtige und privilegierte Boomergeneration, Eure Generation, den Jüngeren ständig vor den Kopf knallt.
10 Warum, das möchte ich Euch jetzt – wie gewohnt logisch (lol) – beweisen. Dafür werde ich Euch natürlich erst einmal erklären, was es mit „OK, Boomer" auf sich hat. „OK, Boomer" (oder „Ok, Boomer" oder „OK Boomer") ist ein Meme, das seit ein paar Monaten im Internet immer häufiger benutzt wird. Ein Meme ist im Regelfall ein humoristisches oder satirisches Bild oder kurzes Video, welches auf
15 eine den Zuschauern bekannte und in dem Kulturraum wiederkehrende Pointe zurückgreift. In diesem Fall ist die Pointe, dass auf unnötig belehrendes, abschätziges oder weltfremdes Verhalten von Boomern schlicht mit einem nüchternen „OK, Boomer" reagiert wird.

Die jüngste Popularität von „OK, Boomer" (oder „Ok, Boomer" oder „OK Boomer")
20 kann in erster Linie auf zwei virale Quellen zurückgeführt werden. Zum einen ist da das Video einer neuseeländischen Parlamentarierin, die während ihrer Rede Zwischenrufe älterer weißer männlicher Kollegen mit einem nüchternen „Okay, Boomer" zum Schweigen brachte. Zum anderen sind da auch virale TikTok-Videos (das ist eine neue Social-Media-Plattform aus China), in denen auf despektierliche
25 Moves von Boomern reagiert wird. Wie zum Beispiel auf einen Boomer, welcher jüngere Generationen in einem ausführlichen Rant angreift und durch falsche Unterstellungen und Verallgemeinerungen schlecht darstellen möchte. In beiden Fällen stellt „OK, Boomer" (und so fort) also eine simple Antwort auf respektloses und geringschätziges Verhalten dar, ohne sich auf das Niveau des Angreifers her-
30 abzulassen. Natürlich gibt es bestimmt auch einzelne Fälle, bei denen der Ausdruck unpassend und unnötig abfällig genutzt wird. Die viralen Trends, der zugrunde liegende Joke und unzählige reichweitenstarke Beispiele tun dies allerdings nicht.

Dass dennoch manche (!) Boomer allein durch diese Bezeichnung ein flaues
35 Gefühl im Magen bekommen, hat viel eher etwas mit dem Verlust des Status quo im öffentlichen Diskurs zu tun. Für alle anderen Generationen ist es völlig normal, dass über sie als Gruppe gesprochen wird. Zeitungen denken und sprechen meist aus der Perspektive der Alten, die für die Jungen irgendwelche Labels wie „Millennials" oder „Gen Z" erfinden. Wenn Boomer die Zeitung dann zuschlagen
40 und den Fernseher anmachen, erfahren sie die Einordnung der aktuellen Themen von Influencerinnen wie Sandra Maischberger (Boomerin), Frank Plasberg

> **Info**
> **Rezo** (born 1992) is a German vlogger and social media influencer. He publishes on his video channels and is well known for his outspoken political criticism.

▶ More info

Text 3/4

(Boomer), Anne Will (Boomerin), Maybrit Illner (Boomerin) oder Markus Lanz (Boomer). Der ZDF-Fernsehrat – nur als Beispiel für den öffentlich-rechtlichen Rundfunk – besteht zu 58 Prozent aus Boomern und neben dieser Gruppe gibt es
45 mehr Mitglieder im gesetzlichen Rentenalter als Mitglieder unter 50 Jahren. Fun Fact am Rande: Der ZDF-Fernsehrat beschreibt seine Mitglieder als „so vielfältig wie die Gesellschaft selbst" … lol, OK, Boomer (guckt, so funktioniert das Meme). […]

Am Ende, liebe Boomer, kann ich verstehen, wenn sich „OK, Boomer" merkwür-
50 dig anfühlt. Und es ist nicht cool, wenn Leute diesen Spruch an den falschen Stellen benutzen, um den Gesprächspartner mundtot zu machen. Aber eigentlich sind diese zwei Worte lediglich Ausdruck kollektiver Erschöpfung von Generationen, die durch konstruktives demokratisches Verhalten ständig auf irrationale Politik der Boomer stoßen, deren zerstörerische Folgen nicht die Alten, sondern
55 die Jungen ertragen müssen. […]

Also seht es uns nach, wenn wir einmal zu oft genervt „OK, Boomer" sagen. Es ist ja auch nervig, kein Boomer zu sein. Peace.

From: '"OK, Boomer" ist okay, Boomer!', Die Zeit, 20 November 2019

▶ Getting started 👆

▶ Support p. 26
▶ SF 47: Mediating from German into English, Student's book p. 332

1 `Mediating` You and your English friend hear a young man saying 'OK Boomer' to an older man. Your friend finds this very impolite. Tell him why – according to Rezo – this phrase might have been justified.

Text 4

▶ More info 👆

Someone desirable   Nick Hornby

- What makes somebody desirable? With another student, take turns asking each other the 'This or that' questions below. For any question, you have to pick one of the given options and explain your choice.

  - Call or text?
  - Snapchat or TikTok?
  - Sport or books?
  - Jeans or sweats?
  - Chatting or silence?
  - Introvert or extrovert?
  - Long hair or short hair?
  - Alternative or mainstream?
  - Going out or staying in?
  - Nice friends or nice parents?
  - Mutual hobbies or mutual friends?
  - Good looks or clever conversation?
  - A good sport or an idol on a pedestal?
  - Same taste in music or same taste in food?

In this excerpt from Nick Hornby's novel High Fidelity, *Rob Fleming, the novel's narrator, recalls when he fell in love with Charlie Nicholson.*

I met Charlie at tech: I was doing a media studies course, and she was studying design, and when I first saw her I realized she was the sort of girl I had wanted to meet ever since I'd been old enough to want to meet girls. She was tall, with blonde cropped hair (she said she knew some people who were at St Martin's with some
5 friends of Johnny Rotten, but I was never introduced to them), and she looked different and dramatic and exotic. Even her name seemed to me dramatic and dif-

Annotations
1 **tech** technical college
4 **cropped** very short
4 **St Martin's** college of the University of the Arts in London
5 **Johnny Rotten** (born 1956) stage name of John Joseph Lydon, the singer of the Sex Pistols, a British punk band active between 1975 and 1978

14   Being Young – Joys and Challenges

ferent and exotic, because up until then I had lived in a world where girls had girls' names, and not very interesting ones at that. She talked a lot, so that you didn't have those terrible, strained silences that seemed to characterize most of my sixth-
10 form dates, and when she talked she said remarkably interesting things – about her course, about my course, about music, about films and books and politics.
And she liked me. She liked *me*. *She* liked me. She *liked* me. Or at least, I think she did. I *think* she did. Etc. I have never been entirely sure what it is women like about me, but I know that ardour helps (even I know how difficult it is to resist someone
15 who finds you irresistible) and I was certainly ardent: I didn't make a nuisance of myself, not until the end, anyway, and I never outstayed my welcome, not while there was still a welcome to be outstayed, but I was kind and sincere and thoughtful and devoted and I remembered things about her and I told her she was beautiful and bought her little presents that usually referred to a conversation we had had
20 recently. None of this was an effort, of course, and none of it was done with any sense of calculation: I found it easy to remember things about her, because I didn't think about anything else, and I really did think she was beautiful, and I would not have been able to prevent myself from buying her little presents, and I did not have to feign devotion. There was no effort involved. So when one of Charlie's friends,
25 a girl called Kate, said wistfully one lunchtime that she wished she could find somebody like me, I was surprised and thrilled. Thrilled because Charlie was listening, and it didn't do me any harm, but surprised because all I had done was act out of self-interest. And yet this was enough, it seemed, to turn me into someone desirable. Weird.
30 And, anyway, by moving to London I had made it easier to be liked by girls. At home, most people had known me, or my mum and dad – or had known somebody who knew me, or my mum and dad – when I was little, and consequently I'd always had the uncomfortable feeling that my boyhood was about to be exposed to the world. How could you take a girl out for an underage drink in a pub when you
35 knew you had a scout uniform still hanging in your closet? Why would a girl want to kiss you if she knew (or knew somebody who knew) that just a few years before, you had insisted on sewing souvenir patches from the Norfolk Broads and Exmoor on your anorak? There were pictures all over my parents' house of me with big ears and
40 disastrous clothes, sitting on tractors, clapping with glee as miniature trains drew into miniature stations; and though later on, distressingly, girlfriends found these pictures cute, it all seemed too close for comfort then.
45 It had only taken me six years to change from a ten-year-old to a sixteen-year-old; surely six years wasn't long enough for a transformation of that magnitude? When I was sixteen, that anorak with the patches on
50 was just a couple of sizes too small.
Charlie hadn't known me as a ten-year-old, however, and she didn't know anybody who knew me, either. She knew me only as a young adult. I was already old enough to
55 vote when I met her; I was old enough to

Annotations

9 **strained** nervous, uneasy
14 **ardour** passion, enthusiasm
15 **make a nuisance of yourself** become a source of annoyance
16 **outstay your welcome** stay longer than people want you to
17 **sincere** honest and profound
18 **devoted** loyal and committed
21 **calculation** careful planning of your behaviour in order to achieve your aims
24 **feign sth.** pretend to feel sth.
25 **wistful** with regretful longing
33 **expose sth.** show or reveal sth.
37 **sew sth.** [səʊ] attach sth. with needle and thread
37 **Norfolk Broads, Exmoor** national parks in England
41 **glee** joy, delight
42 **distressing** worrying
48 **magnitude** degree, extent

Text 4

Annotations

56 **hall of residence** university building with rooms for students
61 **fraud** pretender
63 **find sb. out** find out that sb. has a guilty secret or that they have been dishonest / not told the truth
64 **brandish sth.** wave sth.
65 **pack sb. in** (here) end the relationship
67 **St Albans** city north of London
69 **sophisticated** (here) mature

spend the night with her, the whole night, in her hall of residence, and have opinions, and buy her a drink in a pub, secure in the knowledge that my driving licence with its scrambled proof of age was in my pocket ... and I was old enough to have a history. At home I didn't have a history, just stuff that everybody already knew, and that therefore wasn't worth repeating.

But I still felt a fraud. I was like all those people who suddenly shaved their heads and said they'd always been punks, they'd been punks before punk was even thought of: I felt as though I was going to be found out at any moment, that somebody was going to burst into the college bar brandishing one of the anorak photos and yelling, 'Rob used to be a boy! A little lad!', and Charlie would see it and pack me in. It never occurred to me that she probably had a whole pile of pony books and some ridiculous party dresses hidden away at her parents' place in St Albans. As far as I was concerned, she had been born with enormous earrings, drainpipe jeans and an incredibly sophisticated enthusiasm for the works of some guy who used to splodge orange paint around.

We went out for two years, and for every single minute I felt as though I was standing on a dangerously narrow ledge. I couldn't ever get comfortable, if you know what I mean; there was no room to stretch out and relax. I was depressed by the lack of flamboyance in my wardrobe. I was fretful about my abilities as a lover. I couldn't understand what she saw in the orange paint guy, however many times she explained. I worried that I was never ever going to be able to say anything interesting or amusing to her about anything at all. I was intimidated by the other men on her design course, and became convinced that she was going to go off with one of them. She went off with one of them.

71 **splodge sth. around** smear sth. around
74 **ledge** edge of a cliff or windowsill
78 **flamboyance** spectacular extravagance
79 **fretful** uneasy, nervous
85 **intimidated** frightened
91 **intermission** break
95 **slope off** (BE infml) go away without attracting attention
95 **spot** (n) (here) a few cases
99 **come round** come to your senses again
100 **jack in sth.** (BE infml) give sth. up

I lost the plot for a while then. And I lost the subplot, the script, the soundtrack, the intermission, my popcorn, the credits and the exit sign. I hung around Charlie's hall of residence until some friends of hers caught me and threatened to give me a good kicking. I decided to kill Marco (Marco!), the guy she went off with, and spent long hours in the middle of the night working out how to do it, although whenever I bumped into him I just muttered a greeting and sloped off. I did a spot of shoplifting, the precise motivation for which escapes me now. I took an overdose of Valium, and stuck a finger down my throat within a minute. I wrote endless letters to her, some of which I posted, and scripted endless conversations, none of which we had. And when I came round, after a couple of months of darkness, I found to my surprise that I had jacked in my course and was working in Record and Tape Exchange in Camden.

From: High Fidelity, *1995*

16 Being Young – Joys and Challenges

Text 4

Comprehension

1. Point out how the relationship with Charlie defines the *narrator's identity. Consider the narrator's preoccupation with being a 'fraud' (l. 61).

2. Summarize the narrator's social and emotional development over the episode.

▶ More info

Analysis

3. Examine how the author achieves comic or tragicomic effects. Consider his use of *irony, *register and *repetition.

▶ SF 18: Reading and understanding narrative texts, Student's book p. 286

Language awareness

4. Hornby's text features characteristic aspects of spoken language. Examples are the frequent use of phrasal verbs, interjections, colloquial expressions and repetitive patterns that often rely on stress.

Phrasal verb	Interjection	Colloquialism	Repetition
'turn … into' (l. 28)	'Weird' (l. 29)	'tech' (l. 1)	'girl … meet – meet girls' (ll. 2–3)
…	…	…	…

a Copy the table and fill in further examples from the text.
b Find less colloquial synonyms or rewrite at least two examples from each category in a more formal register.

Beyond the text

5. **You choose** Work on either **a** or **b**.

a **Speaking** After the break-up, the narrator lives through 'months of darkness' (l. 99), before finally dropping out of university. In groups, discuss what could be done to prevent such effects on one's life after a break-up.

b **Writing** Write one of the 'endless letters' (l. 97) the narrator writes in the aftermath of the break-up, either trying to make Charlie feel guilty for your misery or trying to win her back.

▶ Getting started (task a)
▶ SF 44: Having a discussion, Student's book p. 326
▶ SF 36: Creative writing, Student's book p. 311

Language help
It would be essential to … • It might help to … • It would do sb. good to … • Another thing is … • Well, I'd say … • Personally, I think … • If you ask me …

Youth issues: Who am I, and who will I be?

Text 5

Beauty ideals and social media

- Do you share pictures or videos on social media? What do you like about doing this, and what don't you like?
- What topics are trending on social media?

Comprehension

▶ SF 38: Listening/Viewing for gist and detail, Student's book p. 314

Annotations
vain extremely proud of your outer appearance, self-obsessed
roast sb. *(infml)* criticize sb.
catfish sb. *(infml)* trick sb. into a relationship by pretending to be someone else (esp. online)

1 Listening Watch the conversation of six teenagers about posting on social media. Take notes on the following aspects:

- importance of likes
- intentions when posting
- reactions to selfies
- opinions on vanity

Language awareness

2 a Viewing Watch the video again and take notes on nonverbal aspects of communication. Copy the table below and fill in your observations.

Aspect	Observations
Loudness	
*Pitch of voice	
Pauses and speed	
Gestures	
Facial expressions	
Eye contact	

b Examine how these nonverbal elements of communication add to meaning. Give examples.

Beyond the text

▶ Check

▶ SF 30: Writing an (online) article, Student's book p. 304

3 Work on either task **a** or **b**.

a For the English website of your school magazine, you have to prepare an article on beauty standards on social media and their potential risks. Collect and with a partner discuss the main points you want to make. Agree on pictures to illustrate your ideas.

b Challenge Writing Write an article for the English website of your school magazine dealing with beauty standards on social media and their potential risks.

4 Think back to the guiding question and consider if your views have changed, and how.

Being Young – Joys and Challenges

Text 6

Art in Context: 'The fountain of youth'   Lucas Cranach the Elder   ▶ More info

- Talk with a partner: What makes being young attractive and what are the potential benefits of being old?

Then have a look at Lucas Cranach the Elder's painting 'The fountain of youth'.

Lucas Cranach the Elder: 'The fountain of youth', 1546

Comprehension

1. Describe the painting in detail.

Analysis

2. Analyse how the painter manages to capture change in a static picture.
3. Explain the connection between youth, beauty and love implied in the painting. Also consider aspects of gender.

Beyond the text

4. Comment on the interdependence of youth, ideals of beauty and attempts at rejuvenation in this picture and relate it to the situation in modern western societies.
5. Based on your ideas from the pre-reading exercise, describe what a 'fountain of adulthood' might look like.

▶ SF 22: Analysing visuals, Student's book p. 292

Info

Lucas Cranach the Elder (1472–1553) was a German painter and printmaker. He is best known for his portraits of German princes and the leaders of the Protestant Reformation (among them his friend Martin Luther) but also for mythological nudes.

Youth issues: Who am I, and who will I be?   **19**

Text 7

▶ Getting started

Info

William Shakespeare (1564–1616) was an English poet, actor and playwright. He is famous for having written around 39 dramas and 154 sonnets. His sonnets follow a specific structure: in the first 12 lines (three quatrains) an idea is developed or a theory is discussed; the final couplet comes to a conclusion or a surprising turn. The speaker in his sonnets is an old poet.

Annotations
2 **deserts** *(pl)* (here) qualities
3 **tomb** sth. that is built over a place where a body has been laid
6 **graces** (here) elegant assets
8 **touch** *(n)* (here) feature
10 **scorn sth.** reject sth.
10 **tongue** (here) gossip
11 **termed** defined as, considered
11 **rage** (here) wild fantasy
12 **stretched** (here) exaggerated

▶ SF 19: Reading and understanding poetry, Student's book p. 287

▶ Getting started

Eternal youth?

- **Speaking** Work in groups of four and do a placemat activity. Each of you write down three characteristics young people shouldn't lose as they grow up. Then agree as a group on the three most important characteristics.

Partner B: Go to p. 26 and work on the tasks there.
Partner A: Read the text below and work on tasks **1** and **2**.

Sonnet XVII   William Shakespeare

Who will believe my verse in time to come
If it were filled with your most high deserts?
Though yet, heaven knows, it is but as a tomb
Which hides your life, and shows not half your parts.
5 If I could write the beauty of your eyes,
And in fresh numbers number all your graces,
The age to come would say, 'This poet lies;
Such heavenly touches ne'er touched earthly faces.'
So should my papers (yellowed with their age)
10 Be scorned, like old men of less truth than tongue,
And your true rights be termed a poet's rage
And stretchèd metre of an àntique song:
    But were some child of yours alive that time,
    You should live twice, in it and in my rhyme.

From: Sonnets, *1609*

Comprehension

1 Describe
- the concept of youth
- the dangers it faces
- ways to protect it from the dangers

presented in the *sonnet. Be prepared to present the results to your partner.

Analysis

2 a Examine the means Shakespeare uses to get his ideas across. Consider the sonnet's form and language.
  b Choose three major aspects and be prepared to present them to your partner. Bear in mind that they do not know the poem.

3 a Exchange your findings on tasks **1** and **2** with your partner and listen to their findings.
  b Together, discuss how the *stylistic devices in Shakespeare's poem and Dylan's song ensure they remain relevant today.

Text 7/8

Beyond the text

4 With your partner, discuss whether you agree with the *speakers' views on youth presented in the sonnet and the song. You may also refer to your ideas from the pre-reading task and the painting by Lucas Cranach the Elder (cf. p. 19).

5 **Writing** Write a stanza or short poem in response to the song or the sonnet.

▶ SF 36: Creative writing, Student's book p. 311

Text 8

Lifelong lessons?   Emma Jacobs

- Have you ever thought of doing a gap year after school? If so, what kind of gap year could you imagine? If not, why not?

Now read Emma Jacobs's account of her experiences as a gap-year student on a kibbutz in the Israeli desert.

For my generation, rising global temperatures are the norm and a clear threat to our future. [...] So it is important that we explore alternative, sustainable ways to live. That's why I'm spending my gap year learning how to farm in the desert and recycle poo.
5 Yeah, I know, gap yahs have been roundly mocked as the cliched preserve of those privileged youths who just want to 'discover themselves'. But studies have shown they can be good for personal development and teach skills that are beneficial at university and beyond.
So, along with 12 other teenagers, I'm spending a month on Kibbutz Lotan in the
10 middle of the desert in southern Israel. We are a living social experiment: a self-sustaining, ecological 'village'. My home is a dome made of mud, clay, straw and a waterproofing layer of turpentine and recycled cooking oil, which I share with three others. It's a modern hut with a fan, plugs and even air-con. The village has compost toilets, solar showers, a sustainable kitchen with biogas and a bike-cum-
15 washing machine that provides a work-out.
It's a massive change from the lives that most of us lead back in London. We've replaced Starbucks and shellac nails with shovels; it's taken some time to get over the culture shock.
Our days start with an 8 am wake-up: horribly early for me, but late for the real
20 kibbutz workers who rise as early as 1 am to milk the cows. We start the chores before breakfast: cleaning the kitchen, loos and showers, and 'feeding' the biogas with yesterday's food scraps. After breakfast in the communal dining hall, we have permaculture and ecology lessons about the ethics of genetically modified crops, maintaining compost heaps, caring for the animals and keeping morale up
25 throughout the long, hot days. We shovel goat and cow manure and build mud walls for the kibbutz kindergarten.
Working with animal dung is weirdly liberating for us townies. 'Being on kibbutz has made us feel less materialistic,' says participant Max Klass. He's never worked with animals before but says getting up close to the cows and goats is bringing out
30 his 'rough and ready side'.

Annotations
4 **poo** *(infml)* solid end product of digestion
5 **gap yah** *(humorous)* gap year, i.e. period of time between finishing school and starting university
5 **mock sth.** make fun of sth.
5 **cliched** stereotypical
5 **preserve** *(n)* domain
10 **self-sustaining** maintaining itself independently
11 **dome** hut with a round roof
11 **clay** dried earth, often used to make bricks
12 **turpentine** oil distilled from certain trees
17 **shellac** (here) kind of nail polish
17 **shovel** tool used to move earth
22 **scrap** bit of food left over
23 **permaculture** sustainable agriculture
23 **crop** *(n)* fruit, grain or vegetable won by harvest
24 **morale** good spirit, confidence
25 **manure** waste matter from animals used to fertilize the soil to make plants grow

Text 8

Annotations
31 **feat** great accomplishment
37 **utopia** imaginary perfect world
40 **dairy** building where milk products are processed

A simpler, more sustainable, ecologically ethical lifestyle is an achievable feat if you start on a small scale, adds participant Dan Apter. 'People don't know that shovelling shit is such fun.'

I've found there's more to the kibbutz experience than just an ecological education.
35 We're learning to live a truly communal life. It can be tough, but living in an 'intentional community' feels like valuable training for university and a life of work. Yet even in this utopia, the books have to balance. Like many kibbutzim nowadays, this one has been privatised to ensure its economic survival. But it is still a place where members debate issues such as whether it's ethical to maintain a refet
40 (dairy), the extent of communal responsibility, and how to fairly distribute resources.

This time next year, I'll be at Leeds University. I may not need to pick dates, farm or manage a compost loo there, but I'll take the broader lessons that I'm learning on the kibbutz with me. I know it will affect the decisions I make about all sorts of
45 things, from which products to buy to how to use transport. And it's given me all kinds of ideas for the future.

From: 'Gap year stories: getting a taste of communal living', theguardian.com, 2 January 2017

Comprehension

1 Make notes on the following aspects mentioned in the text:
   1 Two contrasting views on gap years: …
   2 The volunteers' living conditions: …
   3 The volunteers' daily tasks: …
   4 The volunteers' attitude to their tasks:
   5 Topics dealt with in their ecological education: …
   6 The effect that living on a kibbutz has had on Emma: …

Analysis

2 Contrast positive and negative aspects of life at Kibbutz Lotan and examine how their representation supports the author's message.

Language awareness

▶ More language

3 The writer makes frequent use of *informal words or expressions. For example, instead of the standard 'gap year', she uses 'gap yah' (l. 5), which imitates a posh accent and is mildly mocking.
   a Explain the following words and expressions, inferring their meaning from their parts or from their context:
   1 'air-con' (l. 13)
   2 'bike-cum-washing machine' (l. 14)
   3 '[one's] rough and ready side' (l. 30)
   4 'the books have to balance' (l. 37)

   b Find other examples of informal words or expressions and say whether you find them suitable for a quality newspaper like the *Guardian*. Change two of them into a more *formal style and explain how this changes their meaning.

22 Being Young – Joys and Challenges

Text 8/9

Beyond the text

4 You choose Work on either task **a** or **b**.

a Speaking You are a representative of an organization that arranges gap years for students. Prepare and give a talk for a study fair aimed at international students. Make sure to present the benefits of gap years. Refer to Emma Jacobs's account, but add ideas of your own.

b Writing Write an online *article on life after school for your school's website. Discuss the benefits and drawbacks of gap years and present other ideas for the future focusing on your local community.

▶ Getting started
▶ SF 42: Preparing and giving a speech, Student's book p. 324
▶ SF 30: Writing an (online) article, Student's book p. 304

Text 9

Routes into work   Tess Reidy

▶ More info

- Have you already decided on what to do after school? Note down one course at university, one apprenticeship trade and one internship programme that might suit you if you were to launch a career now. Give reasons.
- Compare lists with other students and discuss the reasons for your choices.

Now read the text about the pros and cons of internships, apprenticeships and university courses.

It can feel like there's a lot to think about for job seekers during summer: top employers are on the lookout for interns, grad schemes are available in everything from banking to retail, and with more than 1,500 job roles to choose from, there is a wide range of apprenticeships to consider.
5 To get you focused, here's a myth-busting guide on what to consider before you commit to a career.

Internships don't pay
Unpaid internships are illegal, and most people doing any kind of work experience for longer than two weeks are entitled to the national minimum wage. In fact, law
10 firms, banks and consultancy firms can pay as much as £500 per week for vacation schemes.

Although they typically last for one to three months, there's a growing number advertised for up to a year, and they have become a way to impress employers and figure out what suits you.

15 Unfortunately, many companies still offer them unpaid or run them under the guise of volunteer work. 'In the arts, there is this genuine belief that you are lucky to have one because 100 other people have applied,' says Millie Jones*, 21, who did a four-month unpaid internship for a film festival. 'You can end up doing 16 hour days. I felt I couldn't say no or put my foot down because I didn't want to lose the
20 contract.'

Annotations

2 **grad scheme** *(infml)* = graduate scheme, special employment contract for sb. who has just completed a university course
3 **retail** *(n)* sale of goods, e.g. in shops
5 **myth-busting** correcting false beliefs
9 **be entitled to sth.** have a legal right to sth.
9 **wage** regular payment from employer
10 **consultancy firm** business that offers expert advice
10 **vacation scheme** period of work experience offered to students
15 **under the guise of sth.** taking on the form or appearance of sth.
16 **volunteer** *(n)* sb. who agrees to work without compensation
19 **put your foot down** adopt a strong position

Annotations

23 **do maintenance** perform a caretaker's tasks
29 **solicitor** legal professional dealing with legal documents e.g. for selling buildings
30 **accountant** professional in the financial sector
33 **degree-level** *(adj)* on the same level as an academic degree
33 **incur debt** owe sb. money
37 **craft** *(n)* trade that requires skillful working with hands
42 **offset** beginning
51 **vacancy** job offer
52 **consecutive** following each other directly, without interruption

---

Jones, who was not paid expenses, funded herself with a childcare job at the weekends and evenings. She thinks employers take advantage of people like her. 'One intern ended up doing maintenance round the office, like changing light bulbs,' she says.

Apprenticeships are low-level

People often think apprenticeships are just for specific trades, such as construction, or that they are in some way not academic. This isn't true. They cover a range of sectors and levels. Over the past decade, they have become an alternative to academic education and there are now apprenticeship routes into becoming a solicitor, an accountant, an engineer, or business manager.

According to Stephen Isherwood from the Institute of Student Employers, many high-profile companies now recruit apprentices. 'Apprenticeships offer the opportunity to gain a degree-level qualification whilst working and not incurring student debt,' he says.

You can also end up being the boss. 'A large number of business leaders in the sector are former apprentices themselves', says David Fagan from Make UK, who points out that the average pay for a craft apprentice is £11,000, rising to £20,000 in the fourth year.

Apprentices miss out on the uni experience

True, as an apprentice you'll enter the world of work earlier than your uni mates. You'll also be trained very specifically within a sector, so you need to be dedicated to that from the offset. But this doesn't mean you won't be part of a shared experience. Most organisations take on more than one apprentice, so you will usually have a network of similar aged colleagues.

Corey Bueno-Ballantyne, a mechanical engineering apprentice from Telford, says a big part of going to uni is making friends and you get that from apprenticeships. 'We're together every day, we go out for drinks,' he says. 'We spent our first and second years living together in a hotel.'

Grad schemes are for recent grads

Getting hired is competitive. According to the Institute of Student Employers there are 41 applications for every graduate vacancy. A common misconception is if you don't get one straight away, you've missed out. Plenty of people apply for consecutive years, do a post-university gap year, or even work in a different sector before starting a grad scheme.

'It's likely you'll start your grad scheme with lots of young people who have just graduated, but you don't have to be fresh out of uni to do one,' says Becky Kells, editor of AllAboutSchoolLeavers.

*Name changed for confidentiality

From: 'Internship, grad scheme or apprenticeship – which route into work is best?', theguardian.com, 9 July 2019

Text 9

Comprehension

1 Note down key words on what the text tells us about
  1 internships (4 aspects)
  2 apprenticeships (4 aspects)
  3 grad schemes (2 aspects)

Analysis

2 Analyse the means the writer employs to catch the reader's attention.

Language awareness

3 In order to introduce direct quotes in the text, the writer almost exclusively uses forms of *say* (cf. ll. 17, 24, 34, 36, 45, 47, 56). Rewrite these sentences using more meaningful verbs from the box below.

> point out that … • claim that … • make clear that … • doubt that … • add that … • remember that … • maintain that … • clarify that … • believe that … • concede that

Beyond the text

4 [Speaking] [Intercultural communication] For an international school partnership, you are requested to produce a short informative video clip comparing routes into work in Germany and in an English-speaking country of your choice.
  a Research similarities and differences in both countries, then with a partner agree on the information you want to include.
  b Choose pictures and write the lines of text that convey your ideas.
  c Either make the film clip or draw the storyboard and present it in class.

▶ Check
▶ SF 12: Communicating across cultures, Student's book p. 277

Chapter task

Prepare a short message to your future self, spoken or written, reminding yourself of aspects of young life that should never be forgotten.

▶ Getting started

Youth issues: Who am I, and who will I be? **25**

Support and Partner B

Text 3

▶ p. 14 **Is 'OK, Boomer' ok, Boomer?**

1 Support

List things Rezo criticizes about the Boomer generation and their way of communicating.

Text 7

▶ p. 20 **Eternal youth?**

Partner B

Forever young — Bob Dylan

May God bless and keep you always
May your wishes all come true
May you always do for others
And let others do for you
5 May you build a ladder to the stars
And climb on every rung
May you stay forever young
Forever young, forever young
May you stay forever young

10 May you grow up to be righteous
May you grow up to be true
May you always know the truth
And see the lights surrounding you
May you always be courageous
15 Stand upright and be strong
May you stay forever young

Forever young, forever young
May you stay forever young
May your hands always be busy
20 May your feet always be swift
May you have a strong foundation
When the winds of changes shift
May your heart always be joyful
May your song always be sung
25 Forever young, forever young
May you stay forever young

From: Planet Waves, *1974*

> **Info**
>
> **Bob Dylan** (born 1941) is a famous US-American singer and songwriter who composed music of various genres including Folk, Blues, Rock, Country, Pop and Gospel. The musician became an icon of the civil rights and peace movements in the 1960s due to his songs about racism, social inequality and war. The song 'Blowin' in the Wind' even became a hymn of the protest movement. In 2016 he was the first musician to be awarded the Nobel prize for literature.

Annotations
6 **rung** crosspiece of a ladder
10 **righteous** virtuous, ethical
20 **swift** quick, fast

Being Young – Joys and Challenges

Support and Partner B

Comprehension

1 Describe the concept of youth presented in the song. Be prepared to present the results to your partner.

2 a Examine the means Dylan uses to get his ideas across. Consider the song's form and language.
  b Choose three major aspects and be prepared to present them to partner A. Bear in mind that they do not know the poem.

Now go back to task 3 on p. 20.

Acknowledgements

Cover
stock.adobe.com/Katarzyna Leszczynsk

Photos
pp. 4/5 woman with headphones: Shutterstock.com/insta_photos, volunteers: Shutterstock.com/Dmytro Zinkevych; **p. 5** classroom: Shutterstock.com/Monkey Business Images, protest: Shutterstock.com/Paapaya, basketball game: stock.adobe.com/Marcos, IT job: mauritius images/Rupert Oberhäuser; **p. 6 top**: mauritius images/alamy stock photo/Kuttig – Archival, bottom: mauritius images/Westend61; **p. 7**: stock.adobe.com/Jan H. Andersen; **p. 8** image a: Shutterstock.com/Duet PandG, image b: mauritius images/age footstock, image c: mauritius images/alamy stock photo/Sally and Richard Greenhill, image d: mauritius images/TopFoto, image e: mauritius images/alamy stock photo/BWAC Images, image f: mauritius images/Collection Christophel, image g: ClipDealer GmbH/Andrey Armyagov, image h: Shutterstock.com/WUT.ANUNAI, image i: mauritius images/TopFoto, image j: mauritius images/alamy stock photo/Hager fotografie, image k: mauritius images/alamy stock photo/Sally and Richard Greenhill, image l: stock.adobe.com/Inti St. Clair; **p. 10**: Shutterstock.com/Monkey Business Images; **p. 11**: mauritius images/Image Source; **p. 12**: Shutterstock.com/GaudiLab; **p. 15**: Shutterstock.com/thinkhubstudio; **p. 16**: mauritius images/és collection; **p. 17**: Shutterstock.com/Wachiraphorn Thongya; **p. 19**: Bridgeman Images/Cranach, Lucas the Elder, Fountain of Youth (1546); **p. 20**: Shutterstock.com/ArtMari; **p. 22**: mauritius images/alamy stock photo/Independent Picture Service; **p. 25** top: Shutterstock.com/Monkey Business Images, centre: Shutterstock.com/ESB Professional, bottom: Shutterstock.com/Rawpixel.com

Texts
pp. 10–11: Iqbal, Nosheen. "Generation Z - Are the kids alright?", *theguardian.com*, 21 July 2018, https://www.theguardian.com/society/2018/jul/21/generation-z-has-different-attitudes-says-a-new-report (accessed 30.09.2021), Copyright Guardian News & Media Ltd 2021; **pp. 13–14**: "OK, Boomer" ist okay, Boomer! *ZEIT ONLINE*, Eine Kolumne von Rezo, 20.11.2019, https://www.zeit.de/kultur/2019-11/generationenkonflikt-ok-boomer-millenials-babyboomer-rezo/komplettansicht (Zugriff 23.07.2021); **pp. 14–16**: Hornby, Nick. *High Fidelity*. London, Penguin Books, 2000, pp. 15-17; **pp. 21–22**: Jacobs, Emma and Hickford, Sam. "Gap year stories: getting a taste of communal living", *theguardian.com*, 2 Jan 2017, https://www.theguardian.com/education/2017/jan/02/gap-year-stories-getting-a-taste-of-communal-living (accessed 23.07.2021), Copyright Guardian News & Media Ltd 2021; **pp. 23–24**: Reidy, Tess. "Internship, grad scheme or apprenticeship - which route into work is best?", *theguardian.com*, 9 July 2019, https://www.theguardian.com/careers/2019/jul/09/internship-grad-scheme-or-apprenticeship-which-route-into-work-is-best (accessed 20.09.2021), Copyright Guardian News & Media Ltd 2021.

Song
p. 26 *Forever Young*. Ram-s-Horn-Music/Dwarf Music Sony/ATV Publishing (Germany GmbH), Dylan, Bob